THE
4–7
ZONE

Dr Colman Noctor is a psychotherapist and a lecturer. He is a weekly columnist with the *Irish Examiner*, resident psychotherapist on RTÉ Radio 1's *The Ray Darcy Show* and the author of the parenting self-help title *Cop On*. Originally from Blessington, Colman now lives in Carlow and has three children.

THE
4–7
ZONE

An easy and effective way
to live a balanced life – and
become your own therapist

Dr Colman Noctor

GILL BOOKS

Gill Books

Hume Avenue

Park West

Dublin 12

www.gillbooks.ie

Gill Books is an imprint of M.H. Gill and Co.

© Colman Noctor 2023

978 0 7171 9732 3

Designed by Bartek Janczak

Typeset by Integra Software Services Pvt. Ltd., Pondicherry, India

Edited by Gráinne Treanor

Proofread by Esther Ní Dhonnacha

Printed and bound by CPI Group (UK) Ltd, Croydon CR0 4YY

This book is typeset in 12 on 18pt, Minion Pro.

The paper used in this book comes from the wood pulp of sustainably managed forests.

5 4 3 2 1

This book is not intended as a substitute for the medical advice of a physician. The reader should consult a doctor or mental health professional if they feel it necessary. The identities of the people in case studies in this book, both those who have told their own stories and those whose stories I have told, have been changed to protect the privacy of these individuals.

I would like to dedicate this book to my mother, Brenda Noctor. While I believe I have always subtly implied how much I appreciate my mother and everything she has done for me, I have rarely had an opportunity to state it openly. My mother has been the fiercest ally I have ever had in my life and has always 'had my back'. Although her love has never been conditional, she has instilled in me a value system that I have tried to live by my whole life. She has taught me that the things we achieve have more value when they are earned, and to always be mindful of those who are more vulnerable than us; that we will often be given the choice between what is easy and what is right, and that, when you have the opportunity to do the right thing, you should take it, even if it doesn't feel 'right' at the time. These lessons were not communicated to me through deep and meaningful conversations; they were communicated through role modelling and authenticity. I will never be able to convey to my mother how grateful I am for everything she has taught me and done for me, but I hope this dedication goes some way towards saying how important she has been and always will be to me.

I would also like to make a special mention of my friend Padraic Carter, the man who taught me the true meaning of courage.

Contents

Introduction

My name is Dr Colman Noctor. In addition to being a father of three children and a mental health lecturer, I have a busy psychotherapy practice, facilitate workplace well-being seminars, write a weekly column in the *Irish Examiner* and am a monthly contributor to the *Ray Darcy Show* on RTÉ Radio One. The demand for mental health support has soared in recent years, and I have always tried to disseminate my advice as widely as I can. During the global pandemic that began in 2020, I even took the leap into podcasting, compiling over 30 hours of advice on the *Asking for a Parent* podcast as a resource that anyone could access.

While working in the mental health field over the last 25 years, I have developed a no-nonsense approach to my clinical practice and teaching that tries to incorporate the real-world stories of people I have worked with to inform my understanding of mental health and well-being.

At the heart of my work is the belief that before you address a psychological or emotional issue, you first need to understand it. I try to provide simple explanations for complex mental health problems in the hope that creating a better understanding of the origin of someone's distress will help them to apply the practical solutions they need to manage it.

Over the last few years, we have all had to manage the unprecedented challenges of the global pandemic, climate crises, global conflict and rising inflation. These were, and continue to be, extreme and uncertain times. They often trigger extreme reactions, and negotiating them effectively requires a psychological skill set. Referrals to my psychotherapy practice have soared. In an average week in 2019, I received around five email queries from people looking for support. Since mid 2020, I have been receiving about twenty queries a week, and this does not show any sign of abating.

The main reasons people have for contacting me involve difficulties relating to anxiety. To attribute this to the pandemic would be inaccurate, as anxiety levels in our communities have been rising steadily for over a decade. But this trajectory has not been helped by recent global events. The last few years have been like a proverbial game of snakes and ladders, where we have found ourselves catapulted into isolation and freedom with unsettling regularity. When it came to our mood, anxiety, work, exercise, relationships, alcohol use or eating, it was understandable that our sense of balance was lost.

While trying to offer support to people who were contacting me during this time, I began to recognise a consistent theme in the problems people were presenting with, and there was also a predictability to the advice I was giving them to manage their concerns. It became clear that everyone who was coming

to see me was doing 'too much' of one thing or 'too little' of
something else, and this consolidated for me the importance
of psychological 'balance' and emotional 'equilibrium'.

It is a well-worn mantra that moderation is important
for our mental health, but there is very little direction out
there around how we can achieve and maintain moderation.
Knowing what we need to do and actually doing it are two very
different things.

I was struck by how so many people were struggling to
achieve balance in their lives, and I began to think about the
possible reasons for this trend. It soon became obvious that
our contemporary society endorses anything *but* moderation.
When we sit back and think about it, the constant messaging
we hear, from almost every source, tells us we can 'be anything
we want to be'. The sociocultural narratives drive us to 'make
an impact' and coerce us to 'strive for the extraordinary'.

This powerful narrative normalises excess, and I believe
this is a big part of the problem. What if we are being guided
to follow the wrong map? What if 'the ordinary' is where most
of us need to be?

The belief that we must be extraordinary and make an
'impact' causes us to become consumed with performance and
with validation by others. This has led to hyperinflated expectations, with the result that we believe 'average' is no longer
good enough. At times, average has even become synonymous
with 'bad'.

By definition, average is where most of us will reside. If we associate average with bad, then the vast majority of us will be consigned to a state of discontent, not because our lives are ostensibly bad, but because our expectations have been manipulated and we have lost all sense of 'enough'.

Having a sense of enough is crucial to contentment and essential for us to establish the three core concepts of *self-value*, *self-belief* and *self-worth*. Self-worth is determined by our relationship with ourselves; therefore, a good sense of enough is crucial to creating a healthy relationship with ourselves.

Over the course of my writing, teaching and broadcasting experience, there has been one approach that has received unanimously positive feedback from people I have met. This is the principle of the 4–7 zone, which I believe can help everyone to manage their mental lives a little better. As a result of its popularity and effectiveness, I have tried to capture that approach in this book. The 4–7 zone is not designed just to assist anyone who is struggling with mental health problems – I hope it will also be a support for anyone who is negotiating life's challenges. It is designed to maintain mental fitness in a world that demands psychological and emotional agility, and I believe it has the potential, if used proactively, to manage readers' experiences of stress, perhaps even sparing them the need to attend for psychotherapy.

PART ONE

A Culture of Anxiety: How Did We Get Here?

CHAPTER ONE

A Culture of Anxiety

WHAT IS MENTAL WELL-BEING?

When I ask people what the term 'mental well-being' means or what they understand being 'mentally healthy' looks like, the most common answer I get is 'to be happy'. But when we then talk about what it means to be 'happy', many describe a euphoric image of someone smiling or laughing.

I usually follow this with the question 'How much of your life do you believe you spend, or should spend, happy like that?' The answers are usually that it is somewhere in the 75 to 90 per cent range, and most people are shocked to hear that we probably spend less than 2 per cent of our lives in such a state of euphoric happiness. The reality is that this kind of happiness is a transient experience which, though very pleasant, is quite sparse.

This might sound like a very negative outlook, but if we expect to be smiling and laughing 90 per cent of the time, yet in reality only feel like that 2 per cent of the time, then 88 per cent of the time we are going to feel disgruntled, hard done by or disenfranchised.

Freud supposedly said that 'the most we can hope for is the misery of everyday life'. Admittedly, this does not sound optimistic or chirpy, but in essence it was more accurate than some of the modern-day Instagram slogans that suggest we should be 'living our best life' all the time, which is utterly impossible and misleading.

The most accurate formula for happiness is:

Reality – Expectation = Happiness

The gap between our expectations and reality is the space where unhappiness, anxiety and disgruntlement exist. Unfortunately, there is very little we can do about reality – 'it is what it is' – but what we *can* do is adjust our expectations to try to reduce this gap.

One of the reasons I believe mental distress is so pronounced is that our societal pressures are driving our expectations while our emotional realities are lagging significantly behind. I believe that if we are to attempt to make improvements in our collective mental health, it is not about building more mental health clinics. Instead, it is about trying to stem the societal pressures that are driving our expectations. There is a need to promote a counternarrative that states that 'average is OK', 'discomfort is to be expected', and 'coping skills are developed through coping'.

The flip side of this dynamic is that we tend to pathologise feelings that are not what we expect them to be. By this, I mean that we sometimes interpret worry as 'anxiety' and periods of sadness as 'depression'. There is a well-worn slogan that has gained some traction in recent years promoting the idea that 'it's OK to not be OK'. This was well intended, encouraging people to be open and to talk about their emotional distress. But by the same token, we also need to promote the idea that 'it's OK to be OK' too. This idea of 'OK' is an interesting one, because I worry that it is no longer deemed enough to be OK, and that being OK falls far short of how we expect ourselves to be. However, it is my view that most of our life is spent in the OK range of experiences, and that if we make OK *not* OK, we may be creating a bigger problem than we initially attempted to solve.

So, can I feel sad and still be mentally healthy, and worry and still have a degree of mental well-being? The answer is yes.

An important distinction to make explicit at the beginning of this book is that *not all worry is anxiety and not all sadness is depression.*

We will all experience what could be described as 'mental health problems' or 'mental distress' in our lives. These experiences are a normal part of life and can occur as a result of several life stressors such as bereavement, a relationship breakdown or any stressful event that visits our lives. Inevitably, there are going to be periods when we will feel sad and worried, and this is normal too. These experiences do not mean that we are mentally unhealthy or that we lack mental well-being; they are merely aspects of the human experience of living.

Usually, when we feel worried and sad about something, the support of our family and friends – in addition to our internal coping mechanisms – tends to get us through it. However, when these feelings of worry and sadness do not respond to these supports, but instead continue to persist past a point that would be considered normal, they may evolve into a mental disorder such as anxiety or depression.

When worry and stress persist and don't seem to be responding to the support mechanisms in place, it may well be that our experiences are evolving into 'symptoms' and mental health disorders. However, with no definitive measurement of mental health symptoms, it is up to our observations to determine whether our experiences are problematic or to be expected. It would be convenient if we could do an antigen test for anxiety, or take a blood test for depression levels. But these are not available to us, and so determining the extent of mental distress is completely down to our knowledge of what is normal or abnormal. But 'what is normal' is up for debate.

When people who are experiencing mental distress contact me, they all have the same question: 'Is what I am experiencing normal?' A lot of what I do is concerned with determining what is normal and what is not. The skill set required for this involves being able to assess someone and identify if this is likely to resolve of its own accord, is something that requires some minor adjustments in behaviour or understanding, or is something that requires more intensive intervention. If brought to my attention early, most cases will respond positively to some slight adjustments. However, if something has been festering for a long time, then the more intensive options are almost always required.

What a lot of people do not realise is that it is often not the severity of the distressing experience that determines its classification, but the length of time it has been around. Take grief, for example. To feel distraught and hopeless after the loss of someone dear to you is utterly understandable. However, if this feeling persists indefinitely, then a mental health problem like an 'abnormal grief reaction' may be present.

If you visit a friend who has just had a relationship break-up and they are upset at home, tearful, listening to Adele songs and eating ice cream, you wouldn't call the GP and get a referral to a psychiatrist. Why not? Your friend is tearful, hopeless and unable to function. The likely response is that this is normal given the experience she has just had. However, if you went back to visit her 12 months later and she was still tearful, hopeless, listening to the same Adele songs and eating ice cream, then you might rightly suggest that she needs to see someone. This is not because her symptoms are any different, but because the length of time they have been around suggests she is not coping.

The length of time that something is present and not improving is decisive in determining the extent of the issue. This is where the importance of coping strategies comes into focus. How we cope and respond to adversity is crucially important in determining our mental health outcomes, and is therefore worthy of further exploration.

WHAT ARE COPING STRATEGIES?

'Coping strategies' are what we employ to respond to and survive adversity and maintain perspective. Coping strategies are used when a circumstance demands that we find a way of managing, getting through or processing an event. Our external supports like family and friends are crucial components of coping, but our intrapersonal coping strategies are internal, and so can be a little more complex to understand.

To cope effectively, most situations require a calm and thoughtful approach. This is often hard to access when we are emotionally upset. There is a far greater risk of us 'reacting' rather than 'responding' when we are distressed. If something happens that requires us to cope, it has most likely agitated a negative feeling within ourselves. It may be an event that causes us to feel upset, angry, frustrated, confused or hysterical. These powerful emotional reactions often trigger what is known as the 'emotional mind'. The emotional mind is all about reaction. It is a polarised mindset that often wants to react extremely. When someone upsets us or makes us angry, we often want to banish them from our lives or respond in a dramatic, emotional way that conveys our upset explicitly. However, in almost every situation, the emotional mind is a poor responder. Emotions cloud our judgement, and often a time of crisis is not the best time to make decisions. What is called for is a response, not a reaction.

A response is a measured and thoughtful retort to an emotional situation. Even though the ability to respond may not be accessible in the heat of the situation, we can still employ it after the fact. The response is coming from a place of balance. It has allowed the emotion of the situation to pass and has been able to provide a thoughtful assessment of what is the best course of action.

Chapter Two will introduce the 4–7 zone, outlining how that concept can be utilised to help you to respond rather than react following a reflection on your priorities.

THE RESILIENCE MYTH

Resilience

The capacity to withstand or to recover quickly from difficulties; toughness (Oxford Dictionaries)

'Resilience' is one of the most misunderstood concepts in contemporary language. Resilience is not something you develop because you have had to face hard things that happen to you in your life. It is not the case that the tougher your life has been, the more resilient you will become. Adversity does not determine resilience; resilience determines how we cope with adversity. Resilience is an internal mechanism that is used to respond appropriately and proportionately to the difficulties in our lives. It is about how we can bounce back, manage and process challenging experiences. Resilience is informed by a good relationship with ourselves that contains balance and authenticity, and it is our self-worth, self-value and self-belief that determine our levels of resilience.

Anxiety tries to work in opposition to resilience. It makes us do two things: overestimate the challenge and underestimate our ability. Resilience allows us to put the challenge in perspective and bolsters our belief in our ability by providing us with evidence as to why we can get through this experience. To be resilient, we must seek to put the challenge in perspective and reassure ourselves of our ability. We need to access our reserves of self-worth to dilute the intensity of the experience and bolster our belief in our capacity to manage it. We may have to say to ourselves, 'OK, that didn't go so well, but my life's happiness does not depend on this moment and therefore I must put this challenge in perspective, and I need to remind myself that I'm a good person, that I'm trying my best and that my intentions and choices were the best I could do at the time.' By doing this, we bolster our self-worth and our own ability.

Being able to apply a reasonable perspective and reassure ourselves of our capacity to manage situations is the hallmark of a resilient approach. Resilience is being able to see things for what they are and react proportionately to events. The pillars of being able to apply this approach involve self-worth, self-value and self-belief; and balance and authenticity.

THE LENS THROUGH WHICH WE SEE THE WORLD

What determines our anxiety levels is often our tendency to overestimate challenges, underestimate our abilities, react disproportionately to life events and struggle with our self-worth. All of these factors influence, and are influenced by, the lens through which we see the world.

The importance of this lens cannot be underestimated, as it is crucial to our resilience, our management of anxiety and our relationship with ourselves and others. If we want to become better at coping with adversity, we need to adjust this lens, because it is crucially important to maintaining mental well-being, coping with adversity and developing resilience.

Society plays a role in distorting the lens through which we see the world. Stress is pervasive and prolific throughout our society. Everything we hear, see and experience tends to distort our understanding of our importance and value. Advertisers tell us that if we don't have this particular product, it will be the end of the world: 'If you don't have this deodorant you'll never find a girl'; 'If you don't have this shampoo, your hair is going to fall out.' What society tries to do is to conflate what we *want* and what we *need*. If we're not able to challenge this messaging and distinguish this difference, then we can lose control over our own choices and get confused over what is important and what is not – over our needs and our wants.

It's important to ask the question *Who holds that control over our perceptions?* If we allow advertisers and social media content makers to hold this control, it can make us think that the small stuff is big. The biggest difference in this dynamic in recent years is that our desires and expectations are no longer being manipulated just by advertising companies trying to sell us a product; we are being exposed to our peers doing the same thing. It is no longer a case of us reading celebrity magazines and wishing we lived in Hollywood; now we are looking at our neighbours' Instagram feeds and wishing we had a new fireplace.

The more content we are exposed to, the greater the chance of heightened anxiety and an increase in discontent, and as soon as we lose power over our choices, we lose our capacity to manage anxiety.

OVERCORRECTION IS THE ENEMY OF REGULATION

One of the key aspects of maintaining good mental well-being is 'regulation'. Regulation, by definition, means controlling the rate of something so that it works properly. This process is key to maintaining a physical, psychological and social equilibrium. But equilibrium is not achieved by one extreme action countering a polar opposite extreme action. Such a dynamic creates an 'overcorrection' and a flipping-of-the-dial scenario, where people end up being catapulted between two extremes.

It sometimes seems tempting to try to overcorrect, as we hope that it will undo what we have done before. A classic example of an overcorrection we can all relate to is when someone overindulges in food and drink over the Christmas period and then tries to engage in a strict dieting regime in January. This overcorrection is a classic example of attempting to make dramatic changes that are in most cases unsustainable and inevitably result in 'dysregulation' and failure.

Overcorrection is not new. It can be observed throughout history. If we think about the concept of privacy, there was a time when people were tight-lipped about certain things like their voting habits or earnings, whereas now many seem to divulge almost everything around these issues. Take the subject of sexuality and sexual expression. This was a taboo and repressed aspect of human communication for decades, whereas now there seems to be a theme of oversexualisation in contemporary culture. In many ways, history has always taught us that overcorrections happen and that the dial gets flipped too much in the other direction.

This pattern is evident in human behaviour too. Many of us look to make radical or dramatic changes in our lives, and contemporary culture seems to promote this response. Everything we see is promoting a faster, better way to achieve our goals. But the nature of these faster, better strategies is that they are, more often than not, extreme. They are also shortcuts. Many of us are looking for shortcuts because we have become accustomed to them being available to us. There is no shortage of advertisements for six-pack abs in six weeks, pain relief that gets rid of your headache in four minutes, and five steps to happiness. These shortcuts appeal to our desire for gratification, but they overlook the importance of fulfilment.

The immediacy of the shortcut or the extreme option is appealing because, collectively, we have experienced a lack of patience. This may be in part due to the technology narrative that promotes speed and convenience. The promise of the removal of boredom or waiting is rampant in our societal messaging. The promise of next-day delivery, six-pack abs or a beach body in four weeks is alluring. But this messaging also feeds into our view of ourselves. A lot of the self-help narratives promise a better you. You can have 'more happiness', 'more success', 'more popularity', 'more confidence' or 'more peace of mind'. But all this emphasis on 'more' makes us focus on what we perceive we lack. This book is not a guidebook to *happiness*. It is a guide to not feeling *unnecessarily unhappy*. With all the emphasis on what we lack, we lose our concept of enough, and amid that disorientation, we look to extreme shortcuts to fix it – whatever 'it' is.

The 'it' is important, because when I talk to people who are anxious or sad and ask them about what would help them the most, the answer is often to 'not feel as anxious' or 'not feel so sad'. The answer to these questions may not be to find something external to ourselves to 'make us feel less anxious or sad'. Perhaps it is to reframe the experiences that we feel are causing our anxiety or sadness.

All success and failure are subject to perception. What we base our marker for success/failure on will determine our experience of it. It is my view that the baseline markers for success and failure are what are inaccurate, and therefore our sadness and anxiety are related to that problem as much as anything else. I have noticed that many more people are defining success and failure in very concrete terms. It is like there is a belief that success is somewhere between 90 and 100 per cent, and that this is what we all need to aim for. However, this approach by default suggests that everything below 90 per cent is failure, and this belief is distorting our expectations and increasing our feelings of 'falling short'. In reality, success and failure exist on a much more forgiving continuum, and there are many different degrees of success that we need to consider. It is for this reason that our baseline markers for what constitutes success must be determined by each individual and not influenced by the narrative of others. We must have some say in what we determine success to be, what we are happy with, and what we consider failure to be too. This allows us to regain some control over our understanding of contentment and enough.

Of course, this is not the case in every scenario. For people who have experienced genuine tragedy, their extreme emotional experiences are completely rational and not a result of a misunderstanding or distorted expectation. But often what we experience as 'real' is influenced greatly by the world around us. It is well known that our reality is greatly influenced by – and experienced and understood in relation to – the culture and society in which we live. Therefore, it stands to reason that concepts like happiness, sadness and anxiety will be defined by the world around us in a particular moment in time.

Therefore, if I describe myself as 'depressed', I can only do this based on my understanding of what that word means. Likewise, if I describe myself as 'happy', that can only relate to my understanding of what happiness is. Michelle Obama is known for her statement that 'if you can see it, you can be it' when she talks about the importance of female role models. This statement is very true in many contexts. 'If you see it, you can be it' then places a lot of power and influence on what we can see and how we interpret what we see. Therefore, concepts of happiness, sadness and anxiety are dependent upon how those concepts are constructed by our society.

If I were to show you a chair and ask you, 'What is this?', you would most likely say, 'A chair.' Then I might ask, 'Why do you think it is a chair?', to which you might reply, 'Because it looks like a chair and because you sit on it.' If I challenged that by stating, 'But it could also be used as a stepladder to reach something, or a weapon if I threw it at someone, so why do you say it is a chair?', eventually, you might conclude that the only reason why you understood that the object was a chair was because you were told by someone else that it was called a chair.

This suggests that language makes things real, and that many concepts like 'happiness', 'sadness', 'worry' and 'anxiety' are determined by language. Our understanding of language determines our realities and our experiences of them, and therefore it is really important to clarify and challenge the narratives that influence our understanding of concepts. Perhaps the reason we feel unhappy is not that our lives are unhappy, but that the notion of happiness that we have been sold is inaccurate.

Let me explain using the following example.

I was treating a young girl who was referred to me following a very serious attempt she had made to take her own life. It is customary to try to gather a collateral history when you meet someone in a therapeutic setting, to get a sense of the origin of their distress. This young woman seemed to have an objectively idyllic history. She had a loving family and good friends, and she appeared popular and charismatic. She was a strong student at school and a decent sportsperson. Perplexed by the absence of any obvious stressors to explain her unhappiness, I continued to ask some more probing questions about her past. She stopped me and said, 'Colman, my problems are not in my past. They are in my future.' Intrigued, I asked her to elaborate on what she meant by that. She replied, 'What do I have to look forward to in my life? I am going to finish college, get a job, maybe meet someone and have some kids, and die. That's not enough for me.'

At first, I felt somewhat affronted, as this intolerable existence she was describing was almost a direct description of my current life. I asked her to tell me more about it. She described how she felt she had 'already messed up' her life, how she 'hadn't made any impact', and how she doubted she ever would. She described being utterly dissatisfied with the mundane nature of life, saying she needed 'more'. She said she had an 'intolerance of normal'.

My first instinct was to become immediately judgemental of this view. My thoughts ran off about the rise of 'millennial entitlement' and how 'the world has gone mad', but after that momentary internal lapse, I asked her to explain this to me a little more. She went on to explain how she had spent much of her time on social media sites and had been consumed by some of the content there. She had become convinced that she suffered from an 'allergy to boredom', which is something she had come across and which she felt she could relate to. She was told that this affliction affects certain people who are destined for greatness and who cannot tolerate the mundaneness of life. She was convinced that she was destined for a life of dissatisfaction, as she 'was one of those people'. Some of the conversations that ensued had some philosophical references about the meaninglessness of life and the insignificance of being normal, but these perspectives lacked any depth and were more akin to a series of slogans than any coherent perspective.

When I left the session, I was utterly confused. I was not sure how I felt about what I had just heard. There was a risk of becoming dismissive of this girl's situation, as it bore no resemblance to my concept of the world and meaning. However, I spoke about the case in my supervision session, which is where therapists go for therapy, and my supervisor asked me to consider whether my difference in perspective was of any benefit to this young woman's feelings of sadness. When I thought about it, it wasn't. No matter how much I disagreed with the world view this young woman held, the impact of it on her life and perspective was real. Therefore, the risk of her making another attempt on her life was also real. I had to meet this young woman where she was, not where I wanted her to be.

This case highlighted for me how damaging the warped narrative around what we understand as happiness and sadness can be, and how vulnerable we all are to what others determine is enough for us. The volume and transformative impact of these narratives can mean that they influence not only how we see the world, but how we see ourselves. The powerful messaging of promoting shortcuts and selling extremes is negatively impacting the lens through which we see the world, and it is not only the professional influencers that are distorting our world view; we are doing it to each other.

When the world that used to promote the approach of 'expect the worst and whatever happens will be a bonus' flips the dial and overcorrects to 'you can be anything you want to be once you give up the belief that you can't have it', then we have a problem. These are extreme perspectives of the world that are fuelling anxiety, unhappiness and confusion.

This book teaches us how we can take the power back, decide for ourselves what is important, and consequently develop a resilient approach to life's challenges and decide on our 'enough'.

CHAPTER TWO

An Introduction to the 4–7 Zone

LEARNING FROM THE PEOPLE I NEVER SEE

The following paragraphs are an introduction to a strategy that will help you to manage your mental fitness, build your resilience levels and hopefully prevent you from ever needing to attend for psychotherapeutic support. As mentioned in the introduction to this book, I noticed that all the people attending my psychotherapy clinic were doing too much or too little of something, or a combination of both. And I found that in most of the advice I was giving to my clients there was a theme of encouraging them to regain a sense of balance in their lives.

It is common when experiencing difficult or stressful life events to believe that an extreme reaction or response is required. When we are experiencing challenges in our lives, the thought of having to respond to or manage these events is sometimes overwhelming, and so we may choose to ignore the need to make any changes, engaging instead in a state of avoidance. When I was trying to get an understanding of people's struggles, I would ask them to rate their experiences or behaviours out of 10. This allowed me to get a sense of the extent of their behaviours and provided me with some insight into their own perspective on the problem. In some cases, it became clear that people were overdoing an aspect of their lives or underdoing another aspect, or a combination of both, which was compounding their difficulties and, in most cases, making the situation worse.

What became obvious and predictable was that the people who were coming to see me for help to overcome a psychological challenge in their lives were almost always functioning and rating themselves in the 1–3 or 8–10 zones. Nobody who came to me for help rated themselves as functioning in the 4–7 zone. I began to realise there was a pattern which suggested that the 1–3 and 8–10 zones could be understood as 'the danger zones' when it comes to our mental well-being, by default proving that the 4–7 zone was the optimal zone of psychological and emotional safety.

When you take a step back, it makes sense that the 4–7 zone is the safest place to be. When we are engaging in moderate feelings, thinking and behaviour, we are being rational and therefore least likely to become overwhelmed or disengaged. Most people who are experiencing emotional distress find themselves becoming overwhelmed, and engage in either obsessive rumination or avoidant disengagement. And no matter what the origin for the distress is, when the reaction is extreme it tends not to end well.

Many people who are experiencing distress will see their options as polarised and ask which extreme response they should make. Invariably, my answer is that their response should be somewhere in the middle. In the case of 'I am unsure whether this relationship is for me and so I feel compelled to either make it the most perfect relationship ever or break up', the best response is neither of those options. If we are worried about our child's academic performance and we wonder, 'Should I get them a load of grinds, or should we just move to a different school?', again the response is often neither of these polarised options. It may not be news to many people that the moderate response is probably the best option and the one we should strive for, but in many cases, we fail to respond that way. It sounds simple, so why is it so hard?

I believe it is because everything about our culture tends to drive us towards excess, and unrealistically inflates our expectations. The narrative of living your best life, being extraordinary and making an impact is driving us to have unrealistic expectations of ourselves, our lives and other people. These wider narratives are normalising excess. Phrases like 'unlimited', 'all-you-can-eat data', and 'binge watching' are pervasive across society, causing us to lose all sense of enough.

When we are told that every uncomfortable or undesirable situation can be bypassed by a quick fix, it can leave us feeling intolerant of life's ups and downs and compelled to try to fix everything. There is an expectation that we should never be bored, tired or unfulfilled, and if we do experience any of these things, then there is a life hack available to overcome them. These solutions often involve a dramatic gesture that will bring about monumental changes in our lives and inevitably make us 'happy'.

Unfortunately, our emotional lives do not work well with extremes and shortcuts. The modern-day narrative is driven by the attraction of speed and convenience, and these are not terms that fit well with emotional change. The reality is that life can be difficult sometimes, and uncomfortable emotions are part of the life experience. They have a purpose, and they need to be managed and negotiated, not bypassed or fixed. If we were to believe the extreme mental health narratives we hear, we would all believe that we have a set of mental disorders that require immediate attention. However, as I mentioned already, it is important to realise that not all worry is anxiety and not all sadness is depression. Feeling worried and sad over the course of our life's journey is not only normal and acceptable; it is to be expected. The question is, how do we navigate these experiences successfully?

I believe the 4–7 zone approach is a practical way to help us all to do that, as a strategy aimed at providing us with a template for balance and priority. In a society that normalises excess and encourages us to sweat the small stuff, there has never been more of a need for us to ground ourselves in meaningfulness and solidity. The 4–7 zone will assist us to remind ourselves of our need to recalibrate, achieve a sense of equilibrium and reground ourselves in the aspects of our lives that matter to us.

ACHIEVING MODERATION AND PRIORITY

The first mechanism for achieving a sense of enough is the 4–7 zone. The beauty of this technique is its simplicity, and there are no apps, guides or gadgets needed. A pen and a piece of paper might help, but that's it. The 4–7 zone simply asks you to periodically take a moment out of your day and rate different aspects of your life between 1 and 10.

Over recent years, we have got used to self-testing. Throughout the pandemic, we regularly completed temperature checks and antigen tests to make sure we were physically OK. The same principle was not afforded to our mental well-being, which was also under threat in those times. It was over the course of the pandemic that I got to see the 4–7 zone in action in my own life, and it was my 'go-to' strategy for navigating the pandemic and maintaining a sense of balance, perspective and equilibrium in a period loaded with extremes.

This 4–7 zone was something that a number of my clients referenced as a 'game changer' in terms of managing their mental anguish too. It was this feedback that convinced me that this was something worth sharing with others. If something so simple could have such an extensive impact on people who were struggling so much, then surely it could be something that could be useful to many others. I believe that the 4–7 zone can be incorporated into our lives to assist us in our work–life balance, diet and exercise habits, parenting approaches, social activity and intimate relationships.

HOW DOES THE 4–7 ZONE WORK?

Take a moment to consider any aspect of your life that you are finding challenging or are struggling to negotiate. Then consider the intensity or magnitude of your response to it and rate it out of 10.

If, for example, you are going through a stressful period of your life and you rate yourself in the 1–3 or 8–10 zones of any area of your life, then you have to ask if this response is appropriate or proportionate to this circumstance. Perhaps you are struggling with a sense of being overwhelmed with the demands of your life. When you complete the mental health check, you realise that you are not getting enough sleep (2/10), you are not getting enough exercise (1/10), and your degree of worry and rumination about the stresses in your life is too high (9/10). This quick self-assessment will reveal the problem areas that may be compounding your experience of stress.

Then you need to reflect on how long you have been in these 1–3 or 8–10 zones and try to estimate how long this might need to continue. Some life events are high-octane events and require a 1–3 or 8–10 response. However, if you realise that you have been in the outer zones for a longer period than you should be, or if you realise that the situation does not merit that level of reaction, then you may need to do something to change that.

Often when we feel overwhelmed we react by blaming either ourselves or other people entirely. This is one of the biggest mistakes we can make, because most life circumstances are difficult because of a combination of factors, and very rarely just one.

So, rating our own evaluation or response to the stress is important. If we are stressed because of events in our work life, we may tend to apportion all the blame to ourselves and conclude that we are feeling stressed because we are not good enough. Alternatively, we may apportion all of the blame to other people and feel victimised, therefore believing that everyone is against us. Both responses are in the danger zones of 1–3 or 8–10 and are unhelpful. If your self-criticism is 9–10, then this is an unhealthy response and needs to be addressed, and if your sense of responsibility for the challenges you are experiencing is in the 1–3 zone, this too is equally unhelpful. Despite not always being responsible for the events that occur in our lives, we are always responsible for how we react and respond to them. Therefore, where life stress is inevitable and unavoidable, allowing this stress to impact on our sleep, exercise and self-criticism is utterly influenced by our own responses.

We will inevitably find ourselves in the 1–3 or 8–10 zones, because that's just what life does. The objective of the 4–7 zone is not about avoiding entry into the 1–3 or 8–10 zones. That would be impossible. Life events inevitably cause us to find ourselves there. The important thing is to be able to identify this early and assess whether this is a proportionate reaction to the event and whether the length of time we are spending in the 1–3 or 8–10 zones is sustainable. We then need to try to find a way of getting back to the 4–7 zone as soon as we can. Problems don't arise because we enter the 1–3 or 8–10 zones; they arise when we stay in these zones for too long.

If you can manage to spend most of your time in the 4–7 zone – the mid-range of scores – in terms of your work–life balance, family life, diet, exercise and sleep, and if you aim to 'respond or react' to life events within the 4–7 zone, then the likelihood is that from a mental well-being point of view, all will be well.

HOW IS THE 4–7 ZONE DIFFERENT FROM OTHER SELF-HELP STRATEGIES?

In recent years, we have seen a big movement towards strategies such as mindfulness and meditation when it comes to maintaining our mental well-being. While I can appreciate that many people have found these approaches transformative in terms of their mental health, they are not for everyone.

I have been asked many times why I don't promote mindfulness-based approaches more in my work and writing, and the simple reason is that they don't seem to work for me. Any time I have mentioned this to my colleagues, who incidentally are fans of mindfulness methods, they just tell me I am not doing it right. This may be true, but it doesn't alter the fact that I still don't find them useful.

I have tried these interventions before, but I find that the need to be still and to focus intensely on a sound or sensation makes me more rather than less anxious. I am not a good person for stillness at the best of times. I am always active, and I describe myself as an 'active relaxer'. My way of unwinding or switching off is by playing tag rugby or five-a-side football. During these times, I am thinking about nothing else other than the game. The trials and tribulations of my life are not in my head when I am playing a sport, and so for me it is the perfect distraction.

While I believe we all need some distraction, I have become concerned that almost all of the mental health interventions being promoted at the moment are solely distraction-based strategies. Of course, distraction offers us a temporary and much-needed respite from our overactive, worried minds, but I would question at what point we need to cease distracting ourselves and address the origin of our distress. Some distraction-based interventions seem to inadvertently promote the idea that we should never need to experience emotional pain or discomfort. While I advocate for active relaxation strategies that temporarily remove us from the dimension of worry, they are not a long-term solution. Interventions need to also incorporate some instruction on how to deal with or address the source of our stress.

This is where the 4–7 zone is different. The 4–7 zone works off the principle that worry and stress and emotional discomfort are normal. They are our mind's way of communicating that something in our life is out of balance. They are necessary. It is important to try to not let these emotions get out of hand and dominate our experiences, but it is equally unwise to dismiss, ignore or try to distract ourselves away from them indefinitely. Sometimes we need to tune in to emotional distress and try to interpret what it might be indicating to us. More often than not, emotional distress is made worse by how we think about it, so making alterations to how we think about it is key to resolving it.

The way we tend to think about emotional distress is part of a faulty feedback loop in our brains that makes emotional distress worse. For example, if you get anxious about a pending social engagement, your brain will give you a signal that you are anxious. This often triggers a negative thinking cycle that says, 'I shouldn't feel anxious. I am such a loser for feeling anxious.' Now you are spiralling into a state of being anxious *about* being anxious. This is having a knock-on effect on your self-worth. You may begin to convince yourself that there's something wrong with you. 'Why am I such a loser? Why am I feeling anxious about something so simple? Nobody else gets anxious about these things.' Now you are self-diagnosing that feeling anxious means that you have a deficit or that there is something wrong with you. You begin to focus on what you lack. The spiralling rumination and overthinking are creating more and more anxiety. Distraction-based initiatives could encourage you to focus on something small, like a sound or a sensation, and this grounding might interrupt the rumination loop and allow you to feel calmer. Until the next time.

The 4–7 zone encourages you to take a moment when you start to feel anxious. It does not advocate a distraction away from the source of your worry. Instead, it demands that you question the validity of it. It promotes this validity-testing by introducing context and perspective into the equation. It supports you to access your thinking mind and try to engage in a rational assessment of your emotional mind's experience. It may well be that the social engagement is anxiety provoking and the response you are having, based on previous bad social experiences, is valid. Maybe your experience of anxiety is an appropriate response to the situation. If that is the case, then this spares you from berating yourself for being weak and prevents you from diagnosing yourself as having 'something wrong' with you. Instead, it confirms for you that you are human and that these human responses are understandable. It doesn't suggest that you shouldn't think about the anxious situation anymore. Rather, it suggests you reframe how you are thinking about it.

If, upon reflection, you conclude that your anxious reaction is not warranted and is an overreaction to the impending social event, then you need to challenge the anxious lens through which you are seeing the world. Demand the evidence for why you need to feel so anxious. Reassure yourself that a feeling is not a fact and that the event in question is not the end of the world. Reframe the experience by asking yourself, 'Does my life's happiness depend on this moment?' When the answer is no, then try your best to think differently about your emotional response, accept it as part of the process of living and try to place it within perspective and context. This approach is not *distraction*-based; it is *action*-based.

Accept that this will be difficult the first few times. You are trying to rewire a cognitive pathway, and this is going to take time and practice. Cognitive pathways are powerful things. Think about how you drive your car, brush your teeth or dry yourself after a shower. These are examples of established cognitive pathways. Because you have repeated the same routine over and over again, it becomes automatic. When you drive your car, you do it almost subconsciously. Have you ever bought a new car where the indicators and the window wipers are on a different side from what you were used to in your old car? For the first few weeks, every time it rains, you will signal to turn right, and when you are turning right, you will put on the window wipers. This is the result of a cognitive pathway. Even though you know the operational levers are on the other side, you will continue to automatically reach for the wrong one. Anxious responses are cognitive pathways too, and so they take time to be rewired. The only way you can change a cognitive pathway is by changing the habit. Distracting yourself every time you use the wrong lever won't change the habit; it will only help you to get less upset about making the mistake.

The only way to overcome unfamiliarity is by becoming familiar with something. It is the 'doing' that impacts the 'thinking' and, in turn, the 'thinking' that will impact the emotion. So, when you use the wrong lever in your new car, don't berate yourself for being an idiot and doing the wrong thing. You don't need to pull over and listen to your meditation app for 20 minutes to stop you from getting upset about your mistake. You need to use the other lever, remind yourself that it's hard to get used to something new, and vow to try to get it right next time. Mental fitness is similar to physical fitness. There are no quick fixes, and it just takes time, effort, calmness and consistency for it to begin to work.

CHAPTER THREE

Navigating a Culture of Desire, Excess and Expectation

Why have we started to experience more mental health problems than ever before?

What has changed?

What is different?

It would be unfair to apportion blame for all of the deterioration in our collective mental health to the global pandemic, although it certainly did not help, and it exacerbated many underlying issues. The deterioration in our mental health seems to have predated that, but the combination of an increase in life stressors and reduced access to things we would traditionally have used to maintain our well-being – such as our social supports, sports and hobbies – meant the pandemic was a double whammy in terms of its negative impact on our mental health.

Over the last decade, I have witnessed – possibly as a result of the advent of social media – a surge in our collective expectations. This has included an increase in our expectations of ourselves, our jobs, our relationships and our happiness. The bar at which we can achieve contentment seems to have been driven up and up. That's not unusual. With time, as things tend to improve, our expectations naturally go up. However, there has been a steeper incline in the trajectory of our expectations over the last decade than ever before. I describe this phenomenon as 'the Tinderisation of Society'.

Tinder is a well-known dating app. If we're setting up a Tinder profile, we are encouraged to place great emphasis on the *outward-facing* ego. This means that when we are designing our profile, we're aiming to paint the best picture we have of ourselves. We're trying to think of our most interesting hobbies, our accolades, or the highlights of our lives, as well as that witty one-liner that will hook people in. We are performing in a way that makes us as impressive as we can be.

As the purpose of the online profile is to impress others, it often contains the tangible aspects of ourselves that can be easily measured and compared, and most of all those that are impressive. This emphasis is not surprising, as the outward-facing, performative profile will determine whether we get swiped left or right. So that first impression or that collection of aspects of our life that are impressive will determine how the world will respond and react to us, and how it will engage with us.

Lots of effort goes into the public and outward-facing profile. This outward-facing ego, however, is only a part of who we are. These performative aspects are what we call 'external variables'. They are interactive and *interpersonal*. But there is more to being a whole person than those external variables. As complex human beings, we also have '*internal* variables', which are *intrapersonal* and tend to be the vehicle for how we relate to ourselves. In contemporary society, there seems to be little or no emphasis on the *inward-facing* aspects of ourselves. We tend not to see people describe themselves in terms of their kindness, meaningfulness, purpose, desires, dreams or hopes, because these are of little interest in the profile. We are existing in a world that only values the outward-facing aspects of ourselves. Therefore, it is understandable that these are the parts of ourselves that we concentrate on or value.

This concentration on the outward-facing ego can be witnessed in conversations I have had with a lot of young adults. One sentence that I have heard so many times is 'Colman, I have spent my whole life being who other people wanted me to be, and I forgot to be myself.' This statement captures the great difficulty of the culture in which we live, and demonstrates how the technological world is shaping our mental well-being. The way in which the environment we live in shapes our views, values and expectations is interesting. Social theorists have shown that the interactions of individuals with the world around them give meaning to otherwise worthless things and create the reality of society. It is like what Winston Churchill once said, in a 1943 speech to the House of Lords: 'We shape our buildings, and in turn our buildings shape us.' The impact of online profiles and the evolution of technology has meant that our barometer for what is important and what we need to value is being influenced by the shape of our world.

We now occupy a 'hypercomparative culture'. Through the world of Instagram, Snapchat and WhatsApp groups, we have a view into other people's lives that we never had before. Until recently, we have never been able to compare ourselves with other people so much. But the comparison is often with the highlight reels of each other's lives. Whether it is someone's recent venture into interior design, the flowers they just received from their loving partner, or their child receiving an award for some achievement, contentment with, and the expectations we have of, our own life are shaped by exposure to and sharing of these images and stories online.

The impact of the highlight reel became apparent to me recently with an experience I had with my son. As is a tradition in our house, my son and I watch *Match of the Day* on a Saturday night. *Match of the Day*, for anyone who doesn't know, is a series of highlights of the English premiership games that have been on that day. Recently, I decided to take my son to a live match, and I realised something: despite his seeming enjoyment of the fanfare of the occasion, he found concentrating on the match very difficult. I could see his interest waning the longer the game went on. He was struggling with the aspects of the game that weren't exciting. Because his experience of watching football up to now had been just the highlights, he had never watched a full match where spectators must tolerate all the duller aspects of the game.

Watching him struggle reminded me that we often engage with the world through the fantasy of the highlight reel. And comparing the highlight reel of other people's lives to the 'real-time' version of our own lives can leave us feeling disgruntled with and disenfranchised by our own lives, which seem to be quite mundane and boring in comparison.

Another impact of the performative nature of this situation is that we now seem to value self-confidence more than self-worth. Self-confidence and self-worth are very different concepts. Self-confidence is how you perform outwardly or how you project yourself outwardly into the world. It is very convenient, and it is nice to have, but it's not the same as self-worth, which is more concerned with the way you relate to yourself. It is an inward-facing dynamic. For example, a person might perform well at singing, sports or academics. They engage in these activities in a very confident manner. But that confidence in performance does not have a direct relationship with their self-worth.

The most important relationship any of us will have in our lives is the relationship we will have with ourselves. Therefore, the only truth that matters is *your* truth, and how you critique or evaluate your own experiences is the only opinion that matters to you. This is why the lens through which we see the world becomes so important. If we have a lens that sees the world through highlight reels alone, we run the risk of over-valuing the confidence or performative aspects of life. We risk seeing being self-confident as something to aspire to, undervaluing internal variables of life and dismissing the importance of self-worth. And if our self-worth and self-belief are not at a reasonable level, then we are going to struggle, regardless of how self-confident we feel.

For example, I can give a talk to an audience in an auditorium, and they can all say it was good. They can tell me how much they enjoyed it and give me rousing applause. But if I walk away from the podium believing I was rubbish, then all that feedback from the others is futile. My truth is the only truth that matters, and so if I believe that I was terrible, I might spend the whole drive home crying because I believe that I've wasted people's time. This is why the lens through which we see the world is so important and why we need to do everything we can to keep that lens from being impacted by unreasonable expectations.

It may seem problematic that it doesn't matter what other people say – that what they say will not change what I believe and what I feel. This can leave others around me in a powerless position. However, if all that matters is how we see ourselves, then all the power to change that for the better lies completely with us too, and that should be reassuring. We therefore need to adjust our value systems and our priorities to establish our

concept of enough and not try to live up to or compare ourselves with the enough of others.

If we overvalue confidence, then all the praise and feedback
we get will have little impact on our self-worth or self-belief,
because when people are commenting positively about things
that we are doing, they are in essence praising our performance,
not us. I cannot tell you how many times I have sat in front of a
confident person – possibly an A-grade student or someone who
is flying high in their career. They report having many friends
and a good family, and they are attractive and popular. Their
confidence level is 9/10. Yet they still have a depth of sadness
that doesn't seem to make sense. Others who know them will
say they look as if 'they have everything'. But they don't. When
you explore their experience a little deeper with them, you realise that their self-worth is a 2/10, and therein lies the problem.

When we overly engage in the external variables of our
lives and fail to nurture the internal variables, the confidence/
self-worth balance can be lost. There's no denying that there
is something very gratifying about performing well at something and receiving positive feedback about it. But fulfilment
is a different experience. Fulfilment is more substantial and
nourishing than gratification. Ready-meals can reduce hunger,
but they lack the nutritional value of a home-cooked meal. And
in a similar way to good food nourishing the body, fulfilment
nourishes self-worth.

There's very little moderation as part of the wider narrative
of society. It is an anti-moderation culture. This may also reflect

technological evolution, as the world of technology is all about speed, convenience and gratification. Technology thrives on instantaneous responses and more often than not tends towards the extreme. For online content to go viral, it must be sensational. Moderate is not valued. The online world is driven by what is popular, not what is true, and it has no ethical obligation concerning what is right or true. Instead, it is merely a platform for material. But this is not as harmless as it sounds. It has been proven that algorithms influence the voting habits of certain cohorts, and the internet is consistently impacting our choices, desires and expectations.

Many times, a producer or researcher on a TV show or radio programme has interviewed me about some topic relating to mental health. They have asked me sensational questions like 'Do you believe that mobile phones are the ruination of this generation?' As soon as I express a more moderate response such as 'That's not exactly true', they often respond with 'Thanks for that, we might get back to you,' but they rarely do. Sensational content and views are what the media needs. It's not about moderation or measured debate; it's about polarised views and forcing people to pick a lane. This puts us in a position of 'you are in or you are out', and fuels an 'if you are not with us, then you are against us' mentality that fuels extremist narratives.

I have never heard more references to having to be 'right' and 'left' when it comes to people's political views on things than I have in recent times. This polarised view has emerged because of the value society has placed on gratification, sensationalisation and the normalisation of excess, which mitigates against moderate positioning and moderate responses to world events. Despite these trends having an impact on our own goals for ourselves, they are also impacting the extreme nature of world views and fuelling more and more conflict.

We need to rise above the demonisation of normal and the inability to position ourselves in the middle. Making the moderate position unfashionable also contributes to the current crisis of self-worth. Our belief that we need to be extreme, exceptional or extraordinary directly manipulates our sense of enough, and this has created a collective belief that everyone needs to be 'special'.

Take fulfilment and gratification. Gratification is immediate. It tends to give us a dopamine release hit, which is a pleasant experience. However, much of our emotional life is not about gratification; it is much more closely related to fulfilment.

In an interview with Tom Bilyeu, Simon Sinek brilliantly captured the difference between gratification and fulfilment in terms of intensity and consistency. He explained that you can go to the gym for nine hours in one day, and you will look no different after than when you went in. However, if you use the gym for 30 minutes, three times a week for six months, you will notice a difference. Something like becoming healthy and fit is a fulfilment concept.

Emotionality is very much a fulfilment-based concept too. If we are going to find our sense of enough, it will take time and investment. If we believe that it is a gratification-based concept, we will continue to be manipulated into chasing the 'next big thing' to achieve 'happiness'. But to enter into this game of chasing happiness is to fall for the old trick of chasing rainbows.

Despite most of us knowing there is no 'end of a rainbow', as a rainbow is an optical illusion, some people keep chasing it, believing that there is 'one thing' in life that will bring them happiness. In the same way, just as there is rarely only one reason for people experiencing unhappiness, the reverse is true in terms of happiness. The closest thing to being able to achieve a utopian sense of happiness is to achieve the sense of contentment that happens when we achieve enough. This sense of enough is not static, but will move and evolve, and we have to learn how to move and evolve alongside it.

The illusion that desire and happiness can be sought through material things, or through gratification-based exercises, is powerful, tempting and convincing. This is why we need to take a step back before getting swept up in it. We need to not get caught up in the drive towards excess and expectation. We need to resist being convinced by the narrative that we must be exceptional or extraordinary and that average is bad. We need to reprioritise what is important to us and establish our criteria for our enough instead of trying to follow the criteria of others.

THE DEMONISATION OF 'AVERAGE'

One of the most unfortunate dynamics to emerge in recent years has been that the term 'average' has become synonymous with 'bad' or 'not enough'. I am unsure how and why this has happened, but it is indicative of much of what so many people are struggling with at the moment. The view seems to be that everyone must be 'above average' at everything, and there is a belief system based on the idea that the word 'average' is prefaced with the word 'only'.

If we have collectively decided that 'average' is no longer enough, then we have consigned most of the population to a position of discontent. Most of us will be average at most things – that is central to the definition of average. However, if we want to be among the 10 per cent of the population who are genuinely exceptional, then we have an issue, because the maths doesn't work. If 90 per cent of the population want to occupy 10 per cent of the space on the bell curve, then there are going to be a lot of people who are left feeling unhappy.

The demonisation of the average flies in the face of the 4–7 zone. The 4–7 zone approach not only accepts the average nature of our lives – it *strives* for it. If most of us are striving to be where most of us will eventually end up, then automatically we will be a more content population. Disappointment is always relative to our goals and expectations, and we need to reclaim some influence over where we are and what we are striving for. This means challenging the narrative of 'living your best life' and moving it to 'making the best of your life', sparing us from looking over the fence at everyone else's lives and lamenting the things we don't have. It spares us from having to measure our worth by external things and accolades. It allows us to take back some power in what we want and need, and it rejects those goals that are being set for us by someone else.

The 4–7 zone encourages us to see success and failure on a spectrum. If we have a narrow and immature interpretation of success and see only 9/10 and above as success, then we have a 90 per cent chance of disappointment. However, no aspect of life is as cut and dried as that, especially not in terms of subjective concepts like success and failure. Maybe 9 and above is a top level of success, but 7–9 is pretty good too and needs to be celebrated. And 5–7 is still respectable – there are plenty of options still open to us within that zone. If we find ourselves in the 3–5 zone, this may mean that we need to do some further work but that all is not lost, and 1–3 might be trying to tell us that we need to readjust our expectations or goals, or to start over with a new attitude in mind.

The spectrum of success and failure spares us from catastrophic thinking and helps us to see outcomes as reactions to an effort, and that these outcomes offer us further options, though only if we are open to them. The black and white view of the world that polarises us into 'left' and 'right', 'good' and 'bad' or 'successes' and 'failures' is a convenient and clear way to imagine the world, but it is not reflective of the reality of life's circumstances. Life is grey and emotions are messy, and no matter how much we want to make it concrete and clear, it just doesn't work that way.

Separating the world into good and bad or right and wrong resembles the way a small child sees the world. Children exist in a narrative of 'goodies and baddies' and 'cops and robbers'. These are fantasy positions, and the onset of adolescence usually teaches us that all is not so clear-cut, and that people are decidedly grey. This is a realisation we must all return to, and instead of trying to pigeonhole people into distinct categories, we need to embrace the uncertainty of the middle and accept the greyness that is inherent in the human condition. The 4–7 zone encourages us to see the world through that lens, and supports the idea of the middle as being not only a 'safe place' when it comes to mental well-being, but also a 'secure place' when it comes to our sense of balance and equilibrium.

Applying the 4–7 zone to our lives will help us to take back some agency and control over our own choices. This concept makes us look at things objectively and honestly and identify where we are in our lives. Identifying what you want for yourself will allow you to feel content with the priorities that you choose, rather than your goals being dictated to you by media marketers, influencers, your colleagues or peers.

CHAPTER FOUR

The Six Criteria for a Mental Health Check

Mental well-being is a complex concept. Many factors contribute to good mental well-being and compromised mental well-being. As mentioned earlier, mental well-being is not measurable by any definitive test. There is no X-ray for depression and no blood test for anxiety. Therefore, the assessment of our mental health occurs through a combination of the description of the experience by the individual and the observation of their behaviour and functioning.

To assess our mental well-being, I have developed a useful tool to use to complete a mental health check on ourselves. It helps us to take a snapshot of where we are at in terms of our mental health and in turn measure where we are in the 4–7 zone. The image below depicts the six criteria: the more conscious

or visible dimensions of mental well-being (behaviour, cognition and emotions) on the surface, and the unconscious or less
obvious dimensions (biology, psychology and social) in the
layers beneath.

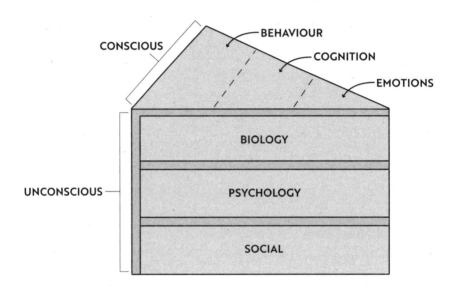

CONSCIOUS AND UNCONSCIOUS
MANIFESTATIONS OF MENTAL DISTRESS

As human beings, we have three dimensions. We think, we
feel and we do. These conscious dimensions of the human
being are indicators as to where our mental well-being is at,
and often any issues that might exist will manifest in these
areas. The other areas where mental distress will manifest
are in our biology/psychology and in our social world, which

are less obvious in terms of their impact or connection to our well-being.

The first and most obvious expression of our mental well-being is what we 'do', in other words, our behaviour, which is the most obvious dimension of the human experience, because we can see and measure it.

Behaviour/Actions

Behaviour includes all the things we do. The most tangible behaviours are our sleeping habits, appetite, energy levels, use of alcohol and degree of engagement with hobbies and other social activities. When our mental well-being is struggling, our behaviours may be the first signpost to there being a problem. Many people can identify that there is a direct impact on their sleep as their stress levels increase. This can result in some people struggling to fall asleep or to stay asleep, while others may oversleep and never feel rested.

The same can be observed in our appetite and diet. When our stress or anxiety levels increase, we might engage in over-eating or comfort-eating or have a loss of appetite. When we are feeling more anxious, we might begin to disengage from social activity too. The result might be that we cancel plans we had made with friends, staying at home alone more, and even isolating ourselves.

It can sometimes be the case that we tell ourselves, 'When I feel better, I will do something different.' In reality, it is often more likely that if you do something different, you will feel better. How we feel affects how we behave, and in turn, how we behave affects how we feel. Our thoughts, feelings and behaviours are all connected, and when our mental well-being is compromised, it will show itself in all three of these areas.

In terms of assessing our behaviours, it's best to first establish a baseline. A baseline is our individual 'set normal'. For example, some people who may be very social individuals may spend most days with other people, friends and family. Others who may be naturally more introverted may spend considerably less time in the company of others. There is nothing wrong or pathological about this, once it is what the person prefers to do. This is not a symptom; it is merely a preference.

When we are assessing our behaviours, we should always compare them to our baseline. If we find that there is some departure from our behavioural baseline, we may need to pay attention to this change. For example, if you find that your aptitude for socialising is quite different from what it usually is, your appetite and diet are changing too, and you are sleeping a lot less than you usually would, then it is time to examine these behaviours through the lens of the 4–7 zone.

If your sleep is 2/10, your diet and appetite are 9/10 and your social habits are 1/10, then it would be important to address these changes. These behavioural indicators could be signs that your mental well-being is starting to struggle, and it is important to try to rectify this pattern as soon as you can. Remember that while temporary excursions into the danger zones of 1–3 and 8–10 are to be expected, it is staying in those zones for long periods that is problematic.

Cognition/Thinking

The next dimension of the human subject that can provide some insights into our mental well-being is our thinking or 'cognition'. This dimension involves our memory, concentration and tendency towards irritability and mental fatigue. When we are experiencing stress or anxiety, we may see this manifesting in our patterns of thought. We may become forgetful or distracted. Our concentration may start to wane and we may also experience difficulties in becoming motivated. These are cognitive aspects of the human subject and can lead to problematic issues of rumination, negative thinking and mental fatigue.

This is more subtle than behaviour and can sometimes be dismissed as 'brain fog' or the result of tiredness. Our thoughts and thinking are incredibly important to our mental well-being. In many ways, they shape how we experience the world. If we are tired and irritable, then we may experience the prospect of going out to meet friends as a chore. We will focus on the negative aspects of the occasion, like the hassle of getting ready and the expense of the event, and create an experience of dread about going out to meet our friends.

At another time, we might experience this event completely differently. If we are cognitively in 'a good place' and are enjoying life, our cognitive lens may well be more focused on optimism. The prospect of the same event is instead experienced as utterly positive. We see it as an opportunity to catch up with friends, we anticipate lots of laughs and fun stories about getting ready, we are excited to show off our new top and shoes, and we are interested to hear what people think of them.

In some circumstances, we can be overly optimistic when it comes to our cognition. If we believe that all our social encounters will be 'amazing' and expect to have 'the best night ever' every time we go out, then we may be expecting a bit too much from life. This overly ambitious optimism can hold life to too high a standard, which can inevitably lead to disappointment and a feeling of disgruntlement. Therefore, it is always important to maintain a degree of balance when we consider the lens through which we cognitively experience the world.

This social example demonstrates the powerful influence of cognition and how it can shape things positively or negatively, depending on how it is functioning. Therefore, a regular assessment of our cognition is important. Thinking patterns can become a habit that can be hard to break. We can carry out this assessment by checking how our thinking, concentration and outlook are in relation to our baseline. If you notice that you are becoming mentally fatigued and experiencing more difficulty than usual with your concentration and memory, this may be an indication that you are coming under cognitive pressure. It is important to try to respond to these changes. Longer-term difficulties with memory, concentration and fatigue can impact our mood and escalate into negative automatic thinking, which can have a significant impact on the lens through which we see the world and lead to anxiety or low mood. It is important to provide our brains and minds with rest, activation or challenge, depending on what is required.

If you rate your concentration as 2/10, your memory as 3/10 and your irritability as 8/10, then there may be a need to rest and recalibrate your cognitive energy. If you are becoming swept up in the culture of expectation and need your work life to be 9/10, your social life to be 8/10 and the degree of fun you experience in your life to be 9/10, you may need to adjust these expectations, as they would appear to be unsustainable and indicate that an inevitable fall is to be expected, which could come at considerable cost and disappointment.

Emotions/Feelings

The most obvious manifestation of our mental well-being comes through the medium of emotion, and our emotions are one of the most difficult dimensions of the human subject to control. They just happen. It is almost impossible to *control* emotion despite what some commentators suggest. What you can do is *influence* emotion, and this is done by changes to your thinking and behaviour.

This is why instructions to 'stop feeling sad' or 'stop being anxious' don't work and are counterproductive. What we need to do when our emotional life is difficult is to try to think differently and reframe emotion, and do things that help us to not let emotion be so dominant over our lives. Emotions are very powerful and can contaminate how we think and what we do, so trying to regain some power over our emotions can be difficult.

Trying to complete a mental health check of our emotions involves looking at how we 'feel' about aspects of our lives. Common powerful emotions include fear, sadness, anger, frustration, euphoria and loneliness. These emotions trigger our emotional mind, which is generally quite reactive and impulsive. The emotional mind does not tend to involve much rationality, and therefore can create a thinking pattern that is quite catastrophic. If you are sad after the loss of a relationship, the emotional mind may try to convince you that you will be alone forever and that you are destined for a life of loneliness and solitude. The emotional power of sadness, loneliness and anger can be hard to manage. These emotions trigger negative thinking styles and rumination – a circular dynamic where 'worst-case scenarios' become inevitabilities. Therefore, the key to managing this intense emotional downward spiral is to try to exercise some changes to how you are thinking about the situation.

Some emotional reactions are warranted, though. Certain life experiences are deeply painful and require an intense emotional reaction. We need to be able to establish some compassion in these situations and allow these intense emotions to exist. The best example of this might be the emotional impact of grief or loss. There is a certain amount of time allocated to individuals who have experienced loss. For example, your employer provides compassionate leave. However, these time allocations are quite arbitrary. It is not possible to allocate six months of grieving time to someone who has lost an immediate family member and one month of grieving time to someone who has lost an extended family member, and yet – unofficially – we do.

This is why we have circumstances of bereavement that are considered 'abnormal grief reactions'. These generally apply to someone who appears to be grieving past the allocated 'normative period'. But how can we place such limits on emotion? We tend not to assess abnormal reactions according to someone's emotional state. Instead, we assess them according to their functioning – that is, their thoughts and behaviours – measured by their capacity to return to functioning in their job, life and relationships. This suggests that the expression of emotion is often only visible through thoughts and behaviours, and so perhaps these dimensions are the best avenues to influence emotional responses. But what is the 'right' emotional response? What is the 'wrong' emotional response? And what does a person who is 'good at emotions' look like? There is a belief that bottling up our emotions and not expressing them is not good for our mental well-being, but being overly demonstrative and expressive of our emotions is deemed unhealthy too. So how do we strike the right balance between expression and suppression of emotion?

There are two types of people in the world when it comes to emotional expression. These are called *internalisers* and *externalisers*. Typically, the externaliser is a demonstrative individual who wears their heart on their sleeve, and they are open about how they view aspects of their life. They are no stranger to an emotional meltdown of tears, anger and vocalised frustration. The internaliser, by contrast, is typically far less expressive. Instead, they tend to mull over or ruminate about their feelings in private. The internaliser is rarely observed demonstrating their emotional discomfort or causing 'trouble', and they are often remarkably compliant and passive.

One might think that the 'internaliser' is what you should strive to be, as internalisers are far less demanding than externalisers. However, in my experience the opposite is true. When I hear a client describe their difficulties as 'a bolt out of the blue' that they 'never saw coming', it always raises my concerns. This is evidence of someone who is not 'tuned in' to their emotions and is unaware of their build-up. This suppression of emotion is problematic, as it prevents people from being proactive in managing emotional build-up and fits the saying that 'you only know how far you can bend when you break'.

I believe that expressing emotion is an essential part of emotional learning. It allows us to test our emotional range and establish how much emotionality we can manage. The process of emotional development, even in adulthood, requires negotiation, argument and voicing your opinion. Belief in your own opinion and value systems reflects a degree of self-worth, self-belief and self-value. Most of my clinical work involves supporting people who are extreme internalisers and extreme externalisers.

Despite the internaliser existing under the radar of friends and family, the prolonged suppression of feelings, or the inability to voice our discontent, is a risk factor for mental health conditions that seem to have control at their core. When we cannot use our voice, or when we feel our expressions are not being heard, we sometimes turn to something else to communicate our distress, such as alcohol, self-harm, eating problems or perfectionism. Contrary to popular belief, agreeableness is not always a healthy quality. So, is externalisation the way to go?

Well, no. Although it is necessary to be non-compliant at times, especially when we need to express our more shadowy emotions, the over-expression of all our negative emotions is not ideal either. Overly externalising all our emotions stems from an inability to contain emotion and can lead to significant problems with emotional regulation and interpersonal relationships. Overexternalisers may exhibit highly emotive responses, which may be impulsive and can do untold damage to their relationships. Acting out all of our emotions can be exhausting and overly dramatic, leading to a high-octane existence that is almost impossible to sustain.

Disagreeableness and disobedience are normative, healthy and necessary, and we run the risk of inadvertently stifling desires by expecting ourselves to behave impeccably at all times. Rather, we need to know that we can survive the odd emotional outburst and manage it if we get on top of it early enough. Having a strop over something that doesn't go your way is emotionally normal, and sometimes being disagreeable is a necessary part of asserting your voice. Someone who can express their desires assertively is more likely to engage in a conversation about the origin of their unhappiness, whereas those who suppress their desire in order to please others will nearly always underplay their discontent and feel misunderstood by the people around them, who they feel seem to miss the point repeatedly.

Much of therapy involves encouraging the expression of emotion, and this has become very in vogue in recent years. However, emotional expression is only useful if it is informed by, or contributes to, the development of emotional intelligence.

Emotional Intelligence

Emotional intelligence is not purely the ability to articulate how something makes us feel. Rather, it is the capacity to be aware of, control and express our emotions, and to handle the emotionality of interpersonal relationships empathetically. This is not simply expressing how we feel; we must also consider the impact of our actions on others – an important aspect of developing empathy and priorities in interpersonal relationships.

Intrapersonal communication involves the internal monologues that we have with ourselves, whereas interpersonal communication involves our interactive communication with others. Emotional intelligence is not simply expressing ourselves; it is also understanding ourselves and our relationships with other people. If emotional intelligence is sold as something too individualistic, we run the risk of it becoming overly self-focused and can lack the consideration of others that is a key social skill and an ingredient for emotional intelligence and emotional resilience.

Encouraging emotional expression but neglecting to develop emotional intelligence can be problematic. Emotional expression promotes the ability to say, 'This is how I feel, and these are my feelings,' but it is also important to develop an awareness of how to understand these feelings and how they impact other people. People with high emotional expression and low emotional intelligence can use social media platforms to vent their feelings, but their expressions can be overzealous, shallow, poorly thought out or overtly hostile, all of which are indicators of high emotional expressions and low emotional intelligence.

To improve our emotional intelligence, we need to develop an awareness of ourselves. We can begin to do this by creating a clearer concept of our values and core beliefs. The ability to identify what is important from what is less important or unimportant allows us to apportion emotion accurately to the aspects of our life that deserve it, and to challenge the allocation of emotion to the aspects of our life that are undeserving of it.

It may help to conceptualise emotions like money. When you are budgeting, you allocate certain amounts to things that you consider a priority – for example, food, shelter, clothes, heat and light. You don't spend your limited funds on luxuries like potpourri or decorative art. This ability to prioritise your spending is understood to be financial intelligence. The ability to do the same with your emotional energy is understood as emotional intelligence. Emotionally intelligent responses are perfect examples of the 4–7 zone, as they are built upon the skills of maintaining balance, equilibrium and priorities.

If you have experienced an upsetting event in your life – perhaps the loss of a relationship – there will be a period when your emotions will be extreme. This might mean that in the aftermath of the event your sadness is 9/10 and your fear of loneliness is 8/10. You might also be experiencing low levels of hope about the future, and your hopefulness might be 2/10. When negative emotions are running high, your thinking may also be extreme. You might think you will never meet someone else, and you might feel intensely angry with the other person because the relationship has ended. These thoughts might also be within the outer zones of the 1 to 10 scale.

Your emotions and thoughts are also likely to impact your behaviour. You may be drinking more alcohol than usual (8/10) and you may be sleeping less than usual (2/10). In this instance, your emotional upset is impacting your thinking processes and your behaviours. It is important to state there is a disclaimer in the 4–7 zone when it comes to alcohol. Alcohol intake is obviously only relevant to the 4–7 zone if you are someone who ordinarily consumes alcohol. Obviously, if someone does not drink alcohol, then the 4–7 zone does not recommend you take up drinking alcohol, and there is no case where an underconsumption of alcohol is problematic. However, it is worthy of inclusion, as it is a major contributing factor to the functioning of many people's mental well-being. Therefore, if someone's consumption of alcohol is in the 8–10 zone for a sustained period of time, it can lead to bigger problems and therefore needs to be highlighted and addressed.

This is what is understood as 'spiralling'. When we spiral, our thoughts and behaviours intensify our emotions. This period of spiralling must not go on indefinitely. After a period of spiralling, it is crucial to recalibrate, and this is done by altering your thinking and behaviours.

Beginning with behaviour, if you consume alcohol and rate your consumption in the 8–10 zone, then it would be advisable to reduce your alcohol intake back within the 4–7 zone, or even lower if possible. You should try to get more sleep and return your sleep score to the 4–7 zone too. In doing this, you will feel more rested and have better clarity of mind. This will begin the process of moving from the emotionally driven mind to the wise mind. As you spend more time in wise-mind thinking, you will start to see that your perspective is shifting. Your hopelessness may become less intense. You may feel more able to socialise with friends again. The return to the 4–7 zone will lead to more perspective on the relationship and allow you to begin to prioritise your own needs again.

Emotions are tricky, because they can be almost impossible to stop or control. We need to work on the way we think about emotions and what we do about them. So, in summary, working on the way we think about emotional upset and trying to do things differently can help us to reframe emotional reactions and formulate an emotional response that is informed by a realignment of our values and priorities and ensures a more proportionate emotional journey.

UNCONSCIOUS

If you have carried out the mental health check on your behaviour, cognition and emotions, there are three more dimensions to the human experience that may also need to be explored. These are the biological, psychological and social aspects of your experience, and they tend to be less obvious in terms of their association with your mental well-being. It often goes unnoticed that our bodies and minds are connected, and we tend to miss the signs that our bodies try to give us when we feel emotionally overwhelmed. The lens through which we see the world and the influence of our social environment on our experiences are also very subtle, and many of us fail to realise the connection and two-way impact these variables have on our mental well-being.

Biology

As with the 'behaviours' mentioned already, we can observe our biology – it is measurable, tangible and visible. There is little doubt that our mental well-being and our physical well-being are connected. We are all familiar with the stomach aches that occur when we have an anxiety-provoking event looming, the neck pain we get when our lives are stressful, or even the reaction of our bowel to life's imminent stressors. If we are not acknowledging the stress in our minds, our bodies will let us know. The best example of this is blushing. When we are embarrassed, our face goes red. Embarrassment is an emotion, and skin changing colour is a physical and anatomical phenomenon, so this proves beyond any doubt that there is an emotional and physical relationship: as we get more embarrassed, our face gets redder, and as embarrassment leaves us, the redness subsides.

Like all things, our mental well-being affects our biology and our biological health, which in turn affects our mental well-being. Our biological markers are like an engine warning light in our cars that tells us our oil level is low or we might need new brake pads, and we ignore them at our peril. We need to remember to listen to our bodies and not run the risk of leaving it too late, when something more serious, like cardiac arrest, might occur.

Psychology

The next dimension is our 'psychological' perspective. This is different from cognition, as it is more concerned with the longer-term lens through which we see the world or our temperament. Temperament is an underdiscussed phenomenon, because we know very little about it and even less about how we influence it. In my therapeutic work, I always try to work 'with' temperament rather than 'against' it. Temperament is quite an enduring and influential aspect of our personalities.

Some people are born with a fiery temperament, whereas others are far more passive; some may have an anxious temperament, whereas others are far more laid-back. This ingrained and pervasive approach to life is an important factor in our mental well-being, as it shapes how we experience things.

I remember buying a new car a few years ago and bringing it up to my parents' house. I was showing my mam all the fancy extras in the car and explaining the way these things worked. When I asked her what she thought, she replied, 'That car will attract thieves to your house.' She couldn't see all the flashy extras as impressive or fancy. Instead, she saw the potential threat. When we are under pressure or experiencing stress, our psychological lens can be affected. If we have experienced a run of disappointments, we may start resigning ourselves to everything letting us down. The way we explain that 'things happen in threes' is an example of how, after an upset or loss, we try to prepare ourselves for inevitable further disappointments. This lens can act as a series of self-fulfilling prophecies and colour how we experience events.

If two people are held hostage for a 24-hour period and later rescued, the impact of the event may be different for each person. One of the hostages may come out of the experience and say, 'I nearly died. Life is too short. I am going to buy that Ferrari, climb Kilimanjaro and embrace my life.' The other person might come out of the same experience and say, 'I nearly died. I am going under my duvet and I am never coming out.' These are polar opposite reactions to the same circumstances, thereby demonstrating the importance of our psychological lens.

It is important to check in with our psychological lens regularly to see if the recent run of experiences is impacting the way we are viewing the world. For example, during the pandemic we learned not to get too hopeful because of the number of false dawns we experienced in terms of vaccines and variants. These experiences can create an outlook of pessimism or hopelessness, which can negatively impact our mental well-being. Equally, a naive psychological outlook that overanticipates that everything will be amazing and work out, without a degree of grounding in realism, is also unhealthy, as it may repeatedly set someone up for disappointment when things don't work out as they anticipated. So, a 4–7 approach to your psychological outlook is crucially important to maintain a healthy, balanced perspective on your life events.

Social

The last aspect of a mental health check is the 'social' dimension. We are all social beings, but some are more social than others. This is not a good or bad thing; it is simply a baseline from which to be able to accurately measure any increases or decreases in our social activity.

Our social lives have undergone a lot of challenges in recent years. The global pandemic altered the patterns of social interaction significantly. Many people got comfortable in the avoidance of social interaction, and that seems to have had long-lasting effects on their socialisation patterns. Social activity is like physical fitness – it needs to be practised to be maintained. In the same way that our physical fitness can deteriorate with lack of activity, so our social fitness can also decline.

Our appetite for social activity can be a good indicator of where our mental well-being is too. When we feel anxious or stressed, social activity can be viewed as a chore to be endured instead of an opportunity to be enjoyed. Also, engaging in social activity can have a significantly positive effect on our mental well-being, and so we need to remind ourselves, as we do with physical exercise, of the importance of keeping our social activity topped up. In the same way that the hardest part of the gym is getting from the couch to the car, the hardest part of socialising might be getting showered and dressed up. When it comes to the gym or the pub, we tend to enjoy it once we get there, and when it's over are often glad that we went.

Social activity can be used as an unhealthy coping strategy too, especially if it is accompanied by alcohol. I can remember one client of mine who had broken up from a relationship and found 'sitting in' alone very difficult as a result. He informed me that he had been coping by going out 29 out of the previous 31 nights. This was most certainly an example of the social scale being in the 8–10 zone, and he was not using his social activity as a coping strategy. Instead, he was using it as avoidance and escapism, and his relationship with alcohol was also at a level that would cause concern.

So, to keep our mental well-being balanced, we need to aim to have our social activity levels within the 4–7 zone. This moderate level of socialising ensures we maintain our social fitness and allows us the opportunity to socially rehabilitate after a stressful or upsetting life event.

The following chapters will explore how we can utilise the 4–7 zone in different aspects of our lives and maintain balance and equilibrium. I will be referring to the six criteria discussed in this chapter to illustrate how we can complete a mental health check and highlight what aspects of our lives may need some adjustment.

PART TWO

The 4–7 Zone: The Sweet Spot Between Too Much and Too Little

CHAPTER FIVE
Work–Life Balance

The issue of work–life balance is something that has come into focus in recent years. This evolution is reflective of how a large majority of people are viewing 'work' differently. It seems reasonable to state that our relationship with our jobs or work has changed considerably in the last two decades, and so it is important to explore why that might be, and what impact it has had on our lives.

If you are within the age bracket of 35 to 55 years old, there is a good chance that your parents were born in the 1930s, 1940s or 1950s. They most likely grew up in the aftermath of the Great Depression and World War II. During that time, there was an understandable obsession with economic security, and people of your parents' generation were raised to build practical and secure careers, with financial security a priority. They too aspired to success, but they had an understanding that to achieve their goals, and for success to materialise, they needed to put in many years of hard work.

Towards the end of the 20th century, many countries entered a new era of economic prosperity and hope. Movies and literature often portrayed themes around 'dreaming big'. This more prosperous time left many feeling gratified and optimistic. With a smoother, more positive life experience than previous generations, the parents of the 1990s raised their children with a new sense of optimism and possibility. Many were attracted by the idea of freedom and equality, including the freedom to accumulate wealth, which some see as epitomising 'the American Dream'.

Around this time, phrases like 'you can be whatever you want to be' emerged in popular culture, instilling a hopeful identity deep within the psyches of children. This seemed to infiltrate the choices children of the 1990s made, and they became optimistic about their futures. Economic security was no longer the only aspiration; there was an emerging desire for fulfilment and a passion within the field of employment and work. This generation needed a lot more from a career than prosperity and security.

What followed was an increase in individual ambition, where the possibility of an 'Individual Personal Dream' was more important than the dream of prosperity. In his book *So Good They Can't Ignore You*, Cal Newport identified the phrase 'follow your passion' as one that became popular only in the last 30 years, at the same time as the phrase 'secure career' became less commonly heard. This 'individual' aspect to the changing narrative was important, because not only did careers have to involve passion and fulfilment, there was an added dimension of 'needing to make an impact' or 'stand out'.

The concept of self-esteem was also something the world of psychology was professing as important, so parents praised their children more openly and found ways to boost their children's self-esteem by giving them feedback about their strengths and qualities. This was all very well for the small child in the school-yard who needed to feel invincible and special, but there was a reluctance to introduce the reality of life as children got older, which would only show its impact at a later stage.

Growing up is a gradual process of disillusionment. When we are four years of age, we believe we are Spider-man, and that's fine. At eight years of age, we begin to doubt this, because other people we know think they are Spider-man too. By 11 years of age, we have to accept that we are not Spider-man, and by 15, when we have acne and feel awkward in almost every social situation, we feel like the furthest thing from Spider-man. This introduction to reality is necessary, and the pace of this intro-duction is really important. If the reality is introduced too early or too harshly, it can put a severe dent in our self-confidence and self-belief, and if it is introduced too late or not introduced at all, it may lead us to have false beliefs about our ability and leave us vulnerable to being hurt by the realities of the outside world.

This can be most pronounced in the workplace, because the funny thing about the world of work is that it turns out to not be an easy place to negotiate, and careers are quite hard. Most take years of blood, sweat and tears to build, and even the most successful people in the world were rarely doing anything that great in their early or mid 20s.

But the hypercomparative culture of social media communication means that we now know far too much about each other, and the capacity to share every aspect of our working lives means that we can't *but* compare ourselves to others with whom we feel we should be on a par. Again, because social media is used in general as a highlight reel of our lives, most people just share their achievements and successes. So, as we scroll through our online social networks, we are bombarded by posts of colleagues achieving promotions, wage increases and employee of the month awards. This echo chamber leads us to believe that everyone must be having a far better experience in their work lives than we are having.

In generations gone by, of course, there were people we went to school with who ended up more successful than we did. We may have heard about this from time to time on the grapevine or at a 10-year school reunion, but in general, we didn't know too much about other people's careers. Now, however, we live in a the 'humble brag' world of social media, where every small achievement is broadcast with all the pomp and ceremony of achieving a PhD.

A comical meme example illustrates this phenomenon, when someone who passes their driving test posts, 'I am honoured and thrilled to announce that I have been selected among the top five applicants who participated in a professional and well-respected exam which evaluates the skills and abilities to operate fuel-based vehicles. I cannot wait to see what the next chapter holds, and cannot express my appreciation to the ministry of transportation, Google and NASA who supported me through this difficult journey.' This comical account reflects the euphemisms that are used to inflate our achievements and make it appear to others that we are excelling in our careers when that may not be the reality. But despite mature reflection telling us that this is the case, we can all get swept up in it. This can leave us feeling unhappy, frustrated and inadequate. Despite most of us probably doing perfectly well in our careers, this dynamic can make us feel like that is not good enough.

LOSING TOUCH WITH 'ENOUGH'

One of the most dominant reasons for our modern-day struggle with our lives is that many of us have lost all sense of enough. The constant exposure to the filtered versions of the lives of others has meant that our standard of enough is determined by others around us. That phenomenon is not new. In times of recession and poverty, having a roof over your head and being able to feed your family might have been considered enough. Like the proverb stating that 'in the land of the blind, the one-eyed man is king', our ability and position in the world are defined by others around us. However, in the last decade, we have seen significant changes in the 'normative', which has had a significant impact on what we consider to be enough.

While we look back on our parents and interpret their experiences of employment to be 'joyless' or 'passionless', we might judge them to have had very poor and unsatisfactory work lives. Back then, not everyone had careers, but many had jobs. My father worked as a warehouse manager for a motor company. I saw him leave every morning and return later that evening, and I never really wondered whether he liked his job or not. He never complained about going to work, and I can remember him dragging himself to work even when he was sick, but he never spoke about how he felt about his job. He just went.

Similarly, my mother was a nurse, and she would leave the house to work the night shift or a 12-hour day, and I never remember having a conversation with her about her experience of her work either. Like my father, my mother rarely missed a day, and attending work was always a highly held value within our family culture. But job satisfaction was not something we ever talked about. In our family, going to work was just something you had to do, and you did it. When I reflect on it now, I would probably guess that my parents' passion for their work was pretty low. I think they saw their jobs as very functional and a means of earning enough money to provide for me and my two sisters. While I admire and appreciate them for doing that for us, I do not think I could approach my work like that now.

Nowadays, we are taught to believe that we need to be passionate about our work and careers. We need to find our work fulfilling and enjoyable. We have been convinced by the mantra that 'if you love your job, you will never work a day in your life', and who wouldn't want that? But how realistic is that? How reasonable is it to assume that we will all be passionate about our work and find all of our jobs fulfilling all of the time? It's utter nonsense. A job or career by its very definition is 'work', that is, 'an activity involving mental or physical effort done to achieve a purpose or result' (Oxford Dictionaries). That is not going to be 'fun' all the time, and it may be the opposite. Our work lives are frustrating, hard, boring, unrewarding and challenging. Even when we think about the more idealistic jobs, like that of a Hollywood actor, it's not all red carpet premieres and chat show appearances. It can involve long periods away from home, having to maintain or achieve certain body shapes for roles, being in the constant glare of the media, hours and hours of rote learning of difficult lines, and never being able to exist with anonymity.

So how do we achieve work–life balance? Should we 'work to live' or 'live to work'? How can we tell whether our work life is enough for us? How do we manage the expectations of our work lives?

The first thing to do when considering whether our approach to our work lives is healthy or not is to complete a mental health check. Take a moment to think through the six criteria – behaviour, cognition, emotions, biology, psychology and social – and relate these areas specifically to your relationship with your job. The relationship that you have with your work life is crucially important, because your truth is the only truth that matters. By this I mean that it doesn't matter what people say you *should* feel about your job; what matters is what you *do* feel. Everyone in your friend group doesn't have to tell you repeatedly how lucky you are to work in a trendy tech company, or your self-employed family members tell you how lucky you are to have a public service job. The only thing that matters when you are exploring your work relationship is how you feel about it. Therefore, you need to apply the 'science of subjectivity'.

JIM

Jim is an accountant in an insurance firm and is responsible for a team of five people. He is good at his job and has received several promotions since starting with the company eight years ago. Jim finds the accountancy aspect of his role fairly manageable. Since he was allocated the team leader position, however, things have got harder. Jim is a conscientious individual who dislikes conflict. He has always been very affable, and would prefer to do without than cause a fuss. This is part of Jim's temperament. For example, if Jim were in a queue in a shop and someone moved in ahead of him, he would be annoyed on the inside but would say nothing. This approach to life means that the team leader role is difficult for him. He likes to be liked by the members of his team so much that he tends to let them away with certain things 'for a quiet life'.

One member of his team is Eoin. Eoin is a younger man and is very popular. He is involved in a lot of sports outside of work and is repeatedly asking Jim for time off to attend training and matches. Jim permits this, but is aware that Eoin's productivity is lower than that of the other members of the team. Rather than create tension in the team, Jim is taking on a lot of the work that Eoin should be doing, on top of his own workload. This is taking its toll on him. He has to work extra hours, and he is very concerned about the impact Eoin is having on the others in the team and how that reflects on his own reputation in the company. Jim has a wife and three small children at home too, and he worries that he is not getting to spend enough time with them. First, let's look at Jim's visible and tangible markers, starting with biology. How is his work life affecting him biologically?

Biology

Jim is currently not sleeping very well, as he lies awake at night worrying about the team dynamics at work. He reports not having had a good night's sleep in over three months. He rates his sleep as a 2/10.

Jim has been to see his GP three times in the last year. This was due to a flare-up of irritable bowel syndrome, psoriasis and recurring chest infections. He would rate his current physical health as 2/10.

Psychology

Jim is not feeling good about himself at the moment. He is angry with himself for not being brave enough to stand up to Eoin. His wife has said he is too much of a pushover and needs to be braver. Jim is anxious about the impact Eoin is having on the team and interprets this anxiety as proof that he must not be able to do his job as team leader. Jim rates his self-worth as a 3/10.

He is constantly braced for the next disaster when it comes to work. He approaches every day with trepidation, worried that the others in the team will 'find out' that he is completing work that Eoin should be doing or that they will revolt against him and report him to his manager, saying that Jim is a poor team leader. Jim would rate his negative thinking style as 9/10.

Social

Jim was never really very sociable, but when we discussed it, he was surprised when he realised that he had not attended a planned social event in over 10 months. The last time Jim was out socialising was for his wife's birthday when they both met with friends for a meal and drinks. Jim enjoyed this event, but has not done anything similar since. He states that this is because it is too complicated to get a babysitter and so it's not worth it. Jim's wife still socialises about every two weeks, but Jim has not got around to organising anything similar with his friends. His friends do meet up, but Jim doesn't go because he has got work to do or he is too tired. When he thinks about going out with his friends, he feels anxious but is not sure why. He rates his social involvement as 2/10.

Behaviour

Jim's activities tend to consist of working and taking his children to and from things. He does not have any hobbies. He used to play golf, but he doesn't have time to do that since the kids came along. His diet and exercise have deteriorated since he started the role of team leader. He generally skips breakfast, survives on coffee during the day, and most nights treats himself to a takeaway meal. He feels he deserves it because he has worked so late. It is his 'only pleasure'. When Jim is working on his laptop late at night, he mindlessly snacks on biscuits and coffee, though he tries to cut down on that because it affects his ability to sleep. Jim's healthy behaviours are 1/10 and his unhealthy behaviours are 8/10.

Cognition

Jim finds that his concentration is poor recently. He has become forgetful, mostly about family commitments. He believes the stress of work is preoccupying him a lot.

Jim describes how he feels as being like 'imposter syndrome'. He believes he is not equipped to do his job correctly and constantly worries that he will be 'found out'.

Jim is finding motivation very challenging at the moment. He states that the only thing he feels motivated to do at the moment is work, but adds that the motivation to put in these hours comes from fear and not desire. He is negatively motivated. Jim's overall cognitive health is a 3/10.

Emotions

Jim reports that he tries to not pay attention to his emotions but that when he does he feels like a failure. He feels very alone in his struggle, because people see him as the team leader and the boss and assume he must be doing fine. Jim feels lonely and misses his friends, but he avoids meeting up with them, because they all talk about how great their work and family lives are, which makes Jim feel worse. Jim feels sad a lot of the time, because he believes he is not succeeding in life. Despite having money, a good job and a loving family, he is still not happy, and surmises that the only reason for this is that he is a selfish person who is never happy. Jim's emotional state is 3/10.

Now let's use the 4–7 zone to illustrate how it can be implemented to improve our work–life balance.

MAKING CHANGES

The first principle that we need to remember is that it is impossible not to veer into the danger zones of 1–3 or 8–10. The inevitability of life means that we will end up there from time to time. The important aspect to pay attention to is the length of time we spend in the danger zones and the severity of the experience. Assessing any problem involves three questions. How severe? How frequent? And for how long? The answers to these three questions will reveal a lot about what changes, if any, need to be made.

The first port of call with any change is always 'action'. We often believe that when we feel better we will do something different. What is more likely, however, is that if we do something different we will feel better. So, with this in mind, the first dimensions of Jim's life that we should focus on are behaviour, biology and social.

In terms of behaviour, Jim rated his healthy behaviours as 1/10 and his unhealthy behaviours as 8/10. So, the first goal is to try to get those ratings back into the 4–7 zone. The first aspect, which is foundational in terms of our well-being, is sleep. Our sleep acts like the battery in our mobile phone. It requires regular opportunities to recharge, otherwise we will find our functioning to be sluggish, glitchy and running on empty. Unfortunately, our bodies don't come with a battery percentage icon, so the management of this is down to the awareness of the person.

We often ignore the signals our bodies are communicating to us because attending to them might be inconvenient. Like Jim's, our physical ailments may well flare up when we are busiest, which is less than ideal. When we are under pressure from work, we are most likely to ignore the early signs of our irritable bowel beginning to grumble, or that tightness across our shoulders coming back again. Instead, we choose to plough on or keep going regardless. However, because we only realise how far we can bend when we break, our bodies tend to send us a more explicit message that can stop us in our tracks, where we can no longer ignore it and must respond. Like Jim, this can lead to more frequent trips to the GP or, in more worrying cases, a trip to the Emergency Department in an ambulance.

Step one for Jim is to address his sleep habits. Although it may be his thoughts that are keeping him awake, his sleep environment is not conducive to good sleep. He needs to improve his sleep hygiene by not working on the laptop after 9 p.m. He needs to reduce the number of sugary biscuits before bed, and he needs to be in bed for the amount of time he hopes to sleep.

The second aspect of Jim's lifestyle that might help get his healthy and unhealthy behaviours back into the 4–7 zone is his diet. All the newest research is suggesting that our diet and activity levels have a monumental impact on our mental health. In Jim's case, it is not about him adopting some severe zero-carbs, zero-everything crash diet. It is simply trying to have three square meals a day at regular times and three smaller snacks in between. Remember, everything about the 4–7 zone is moderate; there will be no recommendations of caveman diets or Ironman-like exercise regimes.

The last aspect of action is social. Jim's social outlets are limited, and he scored his social activities as 2/10. Action therefore needs to be taken to get that up to a 4/10 minimum. Again, there's no need for Jim to go out clubbing five nights a week; simply scheduling something in his diary once a fortnight that involves some degree of social activity and interaction would be all that is required. Our social skills are like muscles; we need to use them to keep them working effectively. The social demands of the workplace are different from the social demands of recreational activity, and sometimes we fail to realise that. We defend against accusations of isolation by saying we speak to people at work every day. But work communication is a different social skill set, and it has a different impact on our self-worth than do more informal and recreational activities. It is important to state that this action does not have to involve alcohol – it could be going to see a football match with a friend, calling over to visit friends or playing a round of golf. It is the beginning of the return to social fitness for Jim, and so small, steady steps are all that is required.

Now that Jim has a better sleeping environment, a more balanced diet and a schedule of activities, the next area of attention is the cognitive and psychological. In terms of his cognition, it is hoped that with improved sleep and diet, and some mental downtime, some of the cognitive cloudiness might lift naturally. But in addition to Jim's cognitive performance of memory and concentration, there is a small matter of his thinking pattern that needs to be explored. Jim rated his negative thinking style as 9/10, and his overall cognitive health and self-worth were both 3/10.

To challenge negative thinking, Jim needs to make some adjustments to the lens through which he sees the world. When he evaluates his self-worth so poorly, who is he rating himself against? Jim is hypercritical of his inability or reluctance to challenge Eoin's work ethic. He is comparing himself to others whom he perceives to be 'good at that', and so is getting into a cycle of being anxious and angry and then becoming anxious and angry *about* being anxious and angry. Maybe no comparison is necessary. Maybe Jim's avoidance of conflict and leaning towards a peaceful existence is not a weakness but a strength. It may not be a strength that is highly valued in his current work environment or role, but that doesn't mean it's not a good thing. In a world that is rife with polarised views, outrage porn and vile and vicious verbal attacks on people who don't share your views, maybe people like Jim are exactly what the world needs. It just might not be what is needed in this particular situation.

Perhaps team leadership is not for Jim. Why must this be a bad thing? Jim was promoted numerous times over his time with the company; he is an excellent accountant. However, this experience may reveal that 'people management' is not suited to Jim and he may not be suited to it. Why must this be viewed as a failure? If you took a professional soccer player and asked him to play rugby, he might be rubbish at it. Does that make him a rubbish person? Of course not. Does it mean he's now a rubbish soccer player too? Of course not. We have ridiculous expectations that we should all be good at everything, and one of the most liberating experiences of your life can be realising that you don't have to be good at everything and owning it.

For years, I struggled with all kinds of administrative work. As a nurse manager and a lecturer, I sucked at it. I didn't think I was rubbish at everything. I knew I was quite good at the teaching and therapy side of things, but note-writing, documenting, policy-writing and governance were not in the repertoire of skills that came easily to me. For years, I ashamedly tried to cover up for these inadequacies at a great cost to my stress levels. I consistently worried about making mistakes in a staff rota, or not submitting the right administrative form, which would result in someone not getting paid on time.

In 2012, I finally decided that these roles were not for me. I owned my deficits, but I diluted them by reminding myself of my strengths. I had progressed in my career at that stage, and I felt less self-conscious that others would judge me for my lack of organisational skill. Instead of negatively affecting my work, this liberated me. I now knew what jobs I was good at and what I enjoyed, and I owned up to my limitations in other roles, trying to work around them. The lens through which I saw the world and myself changed. My experience of exercising some self-compassion was a game changer in terms of my career and job satisfaction. I decided to own up to what I was weak at and tried to focus my energies on other aspects of my abilities that did not make me feel inadequate.

Some might have advocated that the therapeutic work should have involved trying to convince Jim to be more assertive in the workplace – to stand up to Eoin and become more impressive. But that's not what I believed would work. Remember, we have to work with our temperament, not against it. Jim's view of the world is not ideal for his work role, but that doesn't mean that it's 'wrong', so why should I focus on trying to change him? It may not be ideal for the circumstances of his job, but that doesn't mean it's broken or needs fixing. My mother used to say that 'a good run is better than a bad stand', and I think she had a point. What is the point in staying in a set of circumstances that is eroding your self-worth, making you doubt yourself and causing you stress to improve an aspect of yourself that you don't like or enjoy? That doesn't make sense to me. I believe it is sometimes better to own your position and work around it.

By challenging Jim's negative automatic thought association that his struggle with managing Eoin was a sign of his own low value or his 'not-enoughness', I tried to help him to identify that nobody is 'wrong' here; the circumstances are just the wrong 'fit'. I encouraged Jim to challenge his negative automatic thinking and to reframe his experience from one of perceived failure to a circumstance of being the 'wrong fit' for the role. I would expect there are other therapists who would try to support Jim to be able to execute the team leader role more effectively and work on his 'assertiveness', etc. But I have learned over the years that this is not always necessary or desirable. Why should Jim 'fit into' a role that he does not enjoy or find comfortable?

I believe there is a benefit and resilience in accepting our limitations and being comfortable with that, rather than believing that we need to be good at all aspects of our lives. The most important relationship Jim will have in his life is the relationship he will have with himself, and therefore that was the area of my focus for Jim. A good relationship with ourselves involves a degree of self-belief and accuracy about where our strengths lie and an acceptance of where we might not thrive. The acceptance of our limitations, within reason, is a core feature of the 4–7 zone philosophy, and one that protects our mental well-being as opposed to compromising it by our expecting to be excellent at everything. Jim can choose to stay in a role that highlights his perceived deficits and be reminded daily of what he struggles with, or he can act to reframe the experience with context and a different perspective, deciding whether or not he wants to continue in that role.

Many of our career aspirations are not related to the question 'What do you want?', but more accurately they are related to the question 'What are you willing to sacrifice?' Every job involves 'work' that comes at a cost, but instead of asking yourself how hard you are willing to work, perhaps you could ask yourself how much you are willing to sacrifice or suffer. The cost–benefit analysis of Jim continuing in this role may reveal that a request to step out of the team leader role may be advisable. This is not quitting or giving up; it's smart decision-making.

Removing the trepidation of his imposter syndrome and reframing his issues with Eoin as being a mismatch of skills, rather than a deficit in his own value, would improve his cognitive and psychological score. Finding a way out of the role that was causing him so much stress and restoring a healthier sleeping pattern and dietary intake, coupled with a small amount of social and physical activity, could be a game changer for Jim. These changes, alongside being relieved of the role of team leader, could have a significant impact on other aspects of Jim's emotional life. By making these changes, he will feel less alone in his world and less alone in his head, and therefore in a more balanced emotional state.

Like Jim, when it comes to work–life balance we need to break it down and try to address any lack of equilibrium. By acting on the behavioural, biological and social aspects of your lifestyle, you can then begin to explore the cognitive and psychological habits that might be holding you back. In Jim's case, he decided that the team leader role was not for him. He approached his line manager and explained that he felt his talents lay elsewhere and that the role of team leader meant that he was spending more time doing something he felt was not his strength and less time engaged in the role he believed he was better at. Initially, his line manager tried to convince him to give it more time, but Jim articulated how this had been a decision he had reflected on for some time, and how he was confident it was the right move for him. His line manager was convinced by Jim's evaluation and moved him to a different department, where he could continue in a role not dissimilar to the one he had before being promoted to team leader.

The change Jim made to his role might seem somewhat radical, but sometimes when we are in a rut, a radical decision is what is called for. But we lose perspective when our social, behavioural and biological patterns are out of sync. These cloud our ability to make clear decisions and see what is causing us distress. What was important in the case of Jim was his skewed idea of enough. His emotional sadness and fear were driven by a belief that he wasn't enough. But enough in comparison to whom? Jim chose to compare himself with others he believed 'had it all' and didn't struggle with anything. He was trying to be good at something that wasn't him. For whom and for what? Sometimes we need to take a step back and look at the aspects of our lives that are causing us distress and stress and ask ourselves 'why'. A simple assessment of how your work is impacting your life is a useful way to begin the process of addressing the problem.

In Jim's case, he was able to reassess his priorities. Was managing Eoin worth the sleepless nights, the poor health and the lack of time with his family? Here, it is useful to think of 'the Rock/Pebble/Sand Metaphor'.

The Rock/Pebble/Sand Metaphor
This exercise was mentioned in my last book, *Cop On*, and emerged from a story I had heard many years ago involving a philosophy professor.

> A professor entered his classroom with an empty jar. He filled it with rocks and asked the class, 'Is this jar full?' They could see rocks at the top and agreed it was full. Next, he added in some smaller pebbles, which fell in between the rocks, and he filled these to the top too. Again, he asked the class, 'Is it full?' They all saw the rocks and pebbles at the top of the jar and agreed it was now full. Finally, the professor added some sand to the jar. The sand sprinkled between the rocks and the pebbles and filled the jar to the top.

Again, he asked the class, 'Is it full now?' and they all agreed that it was.

The professor explained that the jar of rocks, pebbles and sand represents a fulfilled and meaningful life. The rocks represent the most important things in your life, like your family, health and intimate friendships. The pebbles represent the next layer of important things in our lives, like our job, our performance or our achievements. The sand represents everything else, mostly the cosmetic rubbish that is not that important, like what labels we wear, how many followers we have on social media, etc. The professor explained that the key to feeling fulfilled and achieving meaning was to put the rocks in first, then the pebbles, and then the sand.

The key message in this story is that we need to be able to honestly identify what are the key fulfilling pillars of our lives. This may differ from person to person, and they are largely subjective concepts.

Unfortunately, I believe we live in a world that constantly tells us the sand is important. This is causing us to fill our lives with more meaningless content. As a result, we are 'sweating the small stuff' and losing a sense of what is essential. We must take back control of our own choices. It must be up to us as individuals to choose what 'our' rocks, pebbles and sand are.

This will be different from person to person and will change as we move through different stages of our lives.

Integrating the 4–7 zone and the rock/pebble/sand metaphor in our daily lives will help us maintain moderation and teach us how to prioritise. This will promote our ability to stay grounded and focus on fulfilment instead of gratification. I believe that regularly engaging with these two processes will help us to enhance our resilience, keep us focused on what's important, and defend us from getting whipped up by the storm of expectation and gratification. I still use these techniques, and I believe they have been life-changing in their effectiveness in helping me manage my mental health and that of many of my clients. I believe these are vital tools for anyone who wants to regain control of their choices, preferences and life.

Jim realised that his health and his family were his rocks. His work performance and connections with his peers were his pebbles, and how impressed his colleagues were at his management of Eoin was his sand. Given this realisation of his priorities, Jim made some decisions about his work–life balance that helped him to get back on track. The same could be the case for you.

CHAPTER SIX
Intimate Relationships

Over the many years that I have been facilitating therapy, I have observed the centrality of relationships to our emotional lives. When we consider the aspects of our lives that have the potential to cause us the most acute emotional pain, one of the leading catalysts is loss or disturbances in relationships. The notions of heartache, loss, bereavement and grief are almost always centred around relationships. These can be with intimate partners, family members, friends or pets. A rupture to any of these relationships can cause an emotional pain like no other, which can dominate and severely affect our ability to function and go on. On the flip side, there is nothing that can heal emotional pain like relationships either. They can devastate and obliterate our understanding of meaning in the world, and they can lift us out of ourselves and offer us hope, perspective and purpose in even the most desperate of times. Relationships can be both the most destructive and the most protective elements of our lives.

I have spoken to many people over the years who have experienced dark moments in their lives and contemplated ending it all, only to keep going because of the value of relationships in their lives. When people lose all value in themselves, they can somehow still see the impact of their actions on others, and relationships can be truly life-saving at these times. I have often heard people claim, 'I couldn't do that to my mam/dad/friend.'

If relationships are so crucially important in our lives, and in many ways they sustain us, it is worth spending some time thinking about how we can best nurture and maintain our close relationships and be aware of the issues that can arise in relationships that can put them in jeopardy.

Relationships are formed from the principle of intimacy. We perhaps understand intimacy to be associated with romance or something physical or sexual, and while that is the most common expression of intimacy, it exists in other relationships too. Intimacy is the mutual disclosure of information between people, which over time forms and facilitates a connection or relationship. Without intimacy, a relationship will not evolve, and without a relationship, intimacy will not emerge or be created either.

When we meet someone and begin to form a relationship, it is the degree of mutual disclosure that will determine the depth of that relationship. For example, many of us define close relationships by the degree to which we know each other. This mutual sharing of information creates closeness. But it is not only the quantity of the information that is shared; it is far more about the quality of the exchange. In an intimate relationship, we feel safe sharing our dreams, fears, hopes and anxieties. It is this intimate or private information about ourselves that makes up the currency of the relationship and therefore its depth. Phrases like 'they know me better than I know myself' or 'I can be myself around you' are common, and denote the closeness of a particular relationship. The quid pro quo of sharing intimate information about each other creates a closeness that is rewarding and pleasurable.

As we are innately social beings, we crave safe connections, and so the euphoria created by the closeness of intimate relationships is something we all seek. But sometimes these experiences can be all-consuming. In the early phases of a romantic relationship, where everything is exciting and new, the dynamic between two individuals can often feel special. 'Do you think other people have the connection that we have?' is a common query, and the pleasure of that closeness and safety provides a high almost akin to a drug. This is why we describe these relationships as having 'chemistry' or 'electricity', because they are experienced like a pleasurable high.

However, as with every pleasurable high, tolerance inevitably forms, and it becomes almost impossible to sustain indefinitely. Inevitably, the intensity of the intimacy in the relationship will plateau and we must choose whether to accept the plateau or increase the intensity to maintain the high. The plateauing of intensity is not problematic; it is the natural progression of relationships. However, this is not always how we are sold the idea of what intimate relationships should look like, not only because of the thousands of romantic comedy movies that we have seen, but also more recently because we are viewing the highlight reels of our friends' relationships via our social media networks.

The concept of romantic love and intimacy is a very lucrative business when we consider how many movies, novels and songs are written and consumed on the topic. While we might learn as we get older that the Disney movie character of the prince arriving on a white horse to wake us from our slumber is not a reality, observing our peers receiving flowers and being taken away on romantic city breaks every other weekend is harder to deny. How we understand the concept of intimate relationships will set the expectations we have for our own intimacy goals, and the world of instantaneous gratification and the tyranny of choice can undoubtedly colour our view of what relationships we want in our lives.

The world of dating has changed dramatically too. The impact of online dating apps has drastically changed the dating habits of a whole generation. Again, the concept of choosing a potential intimate partner in the same way as you would choose a pair of shoes is recent. It stands to reason that this may influence the lens through which we see intimate relationships and how we decide what is enough for us when it comes to our choice of partner.

One thing that I have learned through my work as a psychotherapist is that lasting relationships tend to not be extreme. The people who come to me for help with the relationships in their lives tend to have either overly intense and demanding relationships or disengaged and absent relationships. Relationships that exist in these extreme states for too long often run into problems and create emotional pain for those experiencing them.

To illustrate how this can manifest in real-life situations, I am going to give the example of Ellen.

ELLEN

Ellen is a 32-year-old woman who works as a schoolteacher. She was in a long-term relationship with Aaron for most of her late teens and twenties. This relationship was fine, but Ellen began to struggle in her late 20s with the long-term prospects of the relationship. She believed she was content in the relationship, but was worrying about a dilemma that many people face. She thought about how she had been in only one long-term relationship in her life and wondered about whether, if she stayed in the relationship with Aaron, she would turn around at 50 years of age and regret not having 'lived her life' by having more relationships. She then worried about whether, if she ended the relationship with Aaron and 'lived her life', she would later regret that decision and find herself alone at 50 years of age, having given up 'the best thing that had ever happened to her'.

I have heard people struggle with this dilemma as long as I have been a psychotherapist. When people bring this up in the therapy room, they are probably in the wrong room, and perhaps a fortune teller would be a more accurate person to answer their existential questions. What they are looking for is to be able to see the future and use that information to decide in the here and now. As convenient as that may sound, it is not possible, and so the 'work' of this dilemma is trying to figure out your fears, desires and dreams, and decide which of these can be nothing more than a calculated gamble.

In Ellen's case, she and Aaron took 'a break' in the relationship. Within two weeks of taking the break, she heard that Aaron was with someone else. She was devastated. She sought the support of her peers and realised that Aaron had been in this relationship for several months now, and that he was with this other girl while he was with Ellen. She was acutely upset by this news. She felt that all she had known to be safe and true was a lie. She became angry and upset and struggled to function. This acute upset lasted for several months, and just as she was coming to terms with what had happened, she heard that Aaron and his new partner were due to have a baby and planned on getting engaged. This was a further blow to Ellen. She described finding herself under a dark cloud, and she required some time in hospital following an overdose of medication. She has since returned home and is back working and functioning, but has felt 'not herself' ever since.

When Ellen arrived at therapy, it had been five years since the break-up with Aaron, and she described still struggling to 'get her life back on track'. Ellen had described several short-term relationships over the last number of years, but none of them had materialised into anything. She said her friends considered her to be 'too picky', and she agreed. When I asked about these short-term relationships, Ellen described how she tested the people she had met to make sure they would not hurt her, and they had all failed.

When I asked her about these 'tests', she would describe not calling or texting the men she had been on dates with for long periods. She stated she did this to see if they liked her enough, because if they did, they would persist and keep calling or texting. Naturally, this didn't happen, so she believed her tests were working in weeding out the men who would hurt her. On other occasions, when she particularly liked one of the men she was dating, she would tell them very early on in the dating process that she had 'been a patient in a mental hospital and had tried to kill herself', and that if they were going to be with her 'they better be ready to deal with someone like that'. She believed this test was also working, because they had not called her back or asked for another date, so she was right all along and they 'couldn't be trusted'.

This claim of mistrust of the men Ellen was dating was central to her pattern of behaviour. As a result of what happened with Aaron, she had not only lost trust in the potential partners she was meeting, but she had also lost trust in herself. What happens when an intimate relationship involves an experience of betrayal is that the person not only loses trust in the unfaithful person, but they also lose trust in their own judgement. This loss of trust in their judgement can leave them feeling incredibly vulnerable. If we do not believe we have the correct self-protection mechanisms in place, it can be like having to drive a car without any brakes. Not only are we at the mercy of the other drivers, but we are also at the mercy of our capacity to protect ourselves.

As a means of coping with her sense of vulnerability, Ellen was operating within the 1–3 and 8–10 zones. Her commitment to conveying lack of interest and distance to the people she had dated was a 1–3 response, where she disengaged from any contact. Her oversharing of her history and demanding that the person, whom she had just met on a first date, be ready to 'deal with that' was an 8–10 response. Ellen was expecting a long-term commitment level from someone she had just met, which was always going to fail. She was demanding intimacy without a relationship, and intimacy without a relationship cannot exist.

I explained to Ellen that I believed her vulnerability was at the core of her difficulties. The reason she was testing these relationships in such severe ways was because of her fear of feeling vulnerable. The tests she was setting for these men meant they were destined to fail. I explained to Ellen how the principle of vulnerability works using the following metaphor:

> I asked Ellen to imagine a scenario where previously
> she had stood up on a stool to hang up a picture on
> a wall. While she was standing up on it, the stool

broke and she came crashing down. I explained that this stool was like her relationship with Aaron. What she believed was safe and secure turned out not to be. Ever since, she has been fearful of standing up on any stool again. Her experience has left her in disbelief that any stool will support her or is strong enough. Over recent years, it has been as if every potential relationship was like a stool that she needed to test before she felt safe to stand up on it. But instead of testing its robustness by pressing down on it or sitting on it, Ellen was taking a sledgehammer to every stool she came in contact with. Understandably, they all broke into smithereens under that testing regime, and this left Ellen believing that her initial suspicions were indeed correct that ALL stools break and none are to be trusted.

Vulnerability

What the case of Ellen illustrates very well is that there may be very good reasons for our 1–3 or 8–10 reactions to events, and this is why acting outside of 4–7 is not only understandable; it is inevitable. The aim of the 4–7 zone is not to place more pressure on people to get things right all the time; it is about recognising and tuning in to what we are doing, and providing us with the insight to address or correct it. The vulnerability that Ellen experienced was utterly understandable given what she had been through. Many people who have experienced betrayal or trauma will develop a complex relationship with vulnerability. When life takes advantage of our vulnerability, it can make us feel weak.

We can go through life trying to avoid the feeling of vulnerability. I have met many people in my therapy room who have developed an 'allergy to vulnerability'. By this I mean that they react severely to even the slightest hint of potential vulnerability. What a lot of people don't understand is that hope and vulnerability are very closely linked. We only feel vulnerable when we experience something of value that creates fear if there is a risk of potential damage or loss. The only reason vulnerability exists is that we care about something and don't want to lose it. So as soon as we care or hope for something, we are immediately vulnerable. Some people find that feeling of hope intolerable, mostly because they have been let down before.

Many people make decisions throughout their lives to avoid vulnerability. If, for example, you have experienced loss in your life, you may choose to avoid intimacy or closeness in all future relationships. This can lead to a person only superficially engaging in relationships and keeping everyone from getting too close. The mutual sharing of intimate information does not happen, and therefore there is less, if any, chance of being hurt. This might sound appealing to those people who have a fear of being vulnerable or hurt, but the downside to this approach to life is that meaningful relationships are not possible with it, and an inevitable consequence is loneliness. Without vulnerability there can be no closeness, and without closeness there can be no vulnerability.

The work with someone like Ellen involves allowing them to realise that without closeness there can be no vulnerability, but also that without vulnerability there can be no progress. Where Ellen was seeing her past and future intimate relationships as 1–3 or 8–10, she could not cope with the ambiguity or vulnerability of 4–7. And in many cases, 4–7 is a target, not a first step. When I work with someone like Ellen, I am first trying to get them to not see the world solely through the lens of hurt. If your fear of being hurt is 10/10 and your level of trust in others is 1/10, then the goal of therapy in this instance may not be 4–7. Rather, the goal may be to increase the willingness to trust others from 1/10 to 2/10, and over time to allow the fear of being hurt move from 10/10 to 9/10. Vulnerability, by its very nature, needs to be challenged slowly and at a pace that the person can manage. This is why extreme responses to vulnerability tend to backfire.

Remember I talked earlier about not waiting to feel better to do something different, but instead doing something different and then feeling better. The work with someone like Ellen is trying to get her to dip her toe in the pool of vulnerability. It is not about the dramatic gesture; it's about building up her vulnerability tolerance. In a similar way to how you might be desensitised to something you are allergic to, you introduce gradual, small exposures over time. With a bit of luck and a lot of bravery from Ellen, she would slowly allow herself to trust and hope. By creating the possibility for change, change can occur.

These changes are advised so that they offer the opportunity for 'corrective emotional experiences'. These are experiences that help us to productively disassociate emotional feelings from certain circumstances, but they take time. If you have ever got a bad dose of food poisoning after a certain food type, you can create a fear associated with that food, where you actively avoid it. It is only by having small amounts of it over some time and NOT getting food poisoning again that trust can be restored and a new association with that food type can be created. This is a similar pattern to the corrective emotional experience, especially when it comes to intimate relationships and vulnerability.

Now let's use the 4–7 zone to illustrate how it can be used to assess and improve our intimate relationships.

MAKING CHANGES

Biology

When Ellen came to therapy, she was experiencing some biological symptoms of low mood and anxiety. Her sleep was disrupted, her diet was poor and she had low energy levels. Her physical well-being was a 2/10. With small walks during the day, her appetite and sleep improved to a 4/10. She found she had more energy (5/10), and because she was looking after herself better, she noted improvements in her concentration (5/10).

Psychology

Ellen was viewing all future experiences through the lens of her past experiences. She was seeing all potential relationships through the lens of threat. She was unable to see that despite this approach making her feel more protected, it was also making her feel significantly lonelier. Ellen's trust in people was 1/10, and her fear of vulnerability was 10/10. Over time, she began to challenge these belief systems and to look at potential situations through the lens of opportunity instead of threat. She gradually became less defensive and began to allow herself to feel more vulnerable in her relationships. Ellen began this by allowing herself to feel more vulnerable with her friends and to be more honest about how she was feeling. Her friends were supportive and helpful to Ellen, which was a corrective emotional experience for her. It offered an alternative to her belief that 'everyone is out to hurt you'. Ellen began to be able to accept comfort and even to experience some hope in her relationships. With these small changes, Ellen's trust in people improved to a 3/10, and her fear of vulnerability was now 9/10. While still some way off the 4–7 zone, this was still considerable change for Ellen, and it took a lot of bravery on her behalf to achieve it.

Social

Ellen's social contacts had been largely superficial in recent years. Following the betrayal by Aaron, she had lost a lot of faith in other people too. She was convinced that her friends either knew that he was cheating on her and didn't tell her or that her friends must have thought she was a fool to have had that happen to her and for her not to have realised it. As a result, Ellen withdrew from her friendships. While this may not have been obvious in the amount of time she spent with her friends, it was clear in the depth of information she shared with them. Ellen became quieter and more guarded with her friends, not because they had done anything to damage their relationship with her, but rather as a result of the damage that had occurred to Ellen's relationship with herself. She had convinced herself that she was a fool, that nobody liked her and that she was a burden to her friends. So she withdrew from social contact, and her social score was 2/10.

With help and support, Ellen began to try to be vulnerable with her friends again, which allowed for deeper and more meaningful conversations and relationships. When she shared how she felt about herself, her friends were able to understand and reassure her of her value to them. The intimate sharing of fears, hopes and experiences, although agitating Ellen's fear of vulnerability, helped her to feel cared for and loved by her friends. This had a very positive effect on her self-worth and resulted in her socialising more meaningfully. Her social score improved to 4/10.

Behaviour

In terms of her behaviours, Ellen was aware that her approach to dating was not making her feel any better; rather, it was making her feel worse. She subsequently took a break from dating for some time while she worked on herself. She acknowledged that trying to meet someone in the frame of mind she was in was not beneficial to herself or to the men she was dating. Ellen was also drinking almost a bottle of wine per night as a means of comforting herself and helping herself to sleep. This was having a knock-on effect on her mood, and she was feeling quite anxious a lot of the time. She believed that the wine was helping her relax, when in fact it was having the opposite effect. Ellen would have described her healthy behaviours as 2/10.

During her break from the dating scene, Ellen spent time with friends. Although she was anxious about this at first, it soon made her feel really good. She stopped drinking alone and only had wine when she was with others, which improved her mood and anxiety symptoms. Ellen did a series of photography night classes with a friend, which she enjoyed, and she spent some weekends taking pictures for the class the following week. With the reduction in drinking alcohol and the increased social contact, Ellen rated her healthy behaviours as 6/10.

Cognition

Ellen had initially been stuck in a very negative thinking pattern. She described feeling 'unlovable', and the multiple failed dating attempts were compounding this belief. Her self-worth was very low and she was feeling 'useless'. She considered her cognitive health to be 2/10. As she changed her approach to socialising and got some positive experiences with her friends, her self-value improved. With the new experiences with friends and hobbies, she became more future-focused and hopeful. This had a domino effect on her thinking. She was more open to positive experiences. Becoming less fearful of vulnerability also allowed her to experience and think about herself differently. The positive emotional experiences with friends had a significant impact, and she later considered her cognitive health to be 4/10.

Emotions

When Ellen commenced therapy, she was emotionally drained. She had spent years crying and upset about her lost relationship. What had started as anger and fury had evolved into sadness and apathy. Ellen had become indifferent. She had convinced herself that she was doomed or cursed, so she had 'accepted' that she was 'destined to be alone'. Her mood and emotional health were 1/10.

As she made small but significant changes in her social and behavioural habits, you could see things starting to change. Her biological symptoms improved, and she was sleeping better and no longer feeling so nervous all the time. Her experiences with friends allowed her to experience positive emotions, and the laughs they enjoyed were hugely beneficial in improving her emotional world. As Ellen began to test her vulnerability and be honest about how she was feeling with friends, they validated these experiences for her and supported her.

This validation of her emotional pain was a game changer. Ellen no longer had to mask her emotions; she could own them and get some support around them. Sometimes this support was a sympathetic ear, and at other times it was some firm encouragement to act and do something about her situation. No matter what the response, Ellen was grateful for these relationships, as they were authentic. Despite her fears of being destined to be alone, the experience of sharing how she felt emotionally and having that accepted and understood meant that for the first time in years she didn't feel alone. Ellen later suggested her emotional health was 3/10, which was huge for her, considering her baseline starting point.

INTIMATE RELATIONSHIPS

What we need to know about all relationships is that they require work. The illusions created around intimate relationships are unhelpful and unrealistic. When you see someone posting an image on social media of a bouquet of flowers they have just received from their partner, they tend to leave out the fact that the flowers were a form of apology for some indiscretion that happened previously. We are again only privy to the highlight reels of other people's relationships and not the whole story.

But intimate relationships also include experiences that cause you to feel frustrated, when the person you are in a relationship with makes you angry because they are not seeing things the way you see them or they seem too preoccupied to acknowledge your needs. Relationships involve all of these experiences, good and bad. They are fluid and they change. The hope is that they add more to our lives over time than they take away. The goal of lasting relationships is not the constant highs of 8–10 or the dramatic rebounding between 2s and 9s. It is the constant fluctuation through all these zones.

Some relationships will work out, while others will not. There is a belief that when one person's relationship worked out, this means they are a success, and when another person's relationship did not last, this means they have failed. This is simply not true. While there may be clear reasons for relationships breaking down, such as deceit or aggression, most intimate relationships that don't work out fail because of a combination of factors that evolve over time.

The core aspect of culpability must lie in the realm of intent. Very few people enter into a relationship with the intention of it failing. We can only make decisions based on the information we have at our disposal at the time. When things change, relationships change. Most decisions about intimate relationships are made in the 'consensus of the given moment', and this must be part of our internal discussion when we apportion any blame or responsibility for a failed relationship. Oftentimes, we are not responsible for the changes that occur in relationships, but we are ultimately responsible for how we react or respond to these changes, and that is where the 4–7 zone can be useful.

Relationships are partnerships where the bulk of the heavy lifting should not be done by one person all the time. They are 'give and take'. The flow of responsibility may change and the tables will inevitably turn, but our ability to work together provides the relationship with balance and equilibrium, which are essential to its functioning.

The three most common arguments couples have are about money, sex and housework. These are all tasks that demand an evenness or balance so that they do not become problematic. The research and personal experiences would suggest that even in the most healthy or impressive relationships, these issues emerge. So how do we apply the 4–7 zone in something that involves such fluctuation and unpredictability?

As in the case of Ellen, the 4–7 zone does not apply to the events of the relationship but applies instead to our responses and reactions to the events that occur within the relationship. If each member of the relationship can find a way to respond in the 4–7 zone, the likelihood of the relationship's survival is greatly improved. We cannot be responsible for the actions of others, but we are ultimately responsible for our reactions and responses to them. It is the reaction to events in relationships that require a measured response, and although this can be extremely difficult in the moment when emotions are running high – as demonstrated by the case of Ellen – they are effective in our finding our way back to ourselves.

CHAPTER SEVEN
Diet, Sleep and Exercise

All the research in recent years has strengthened the belief that our mental health is closely linked to our physical health. There is growing evidence that the quality of our sleep, diet and exercise are really important to maintaining good mental well-being.

I must admit that I have always been quite cynical of the impact of this supposed link, which I think was more about the people who were promoting the idea than the idea itself. I consider suggesting to someone who is so depressed that they cannot get out of bed that they should go and do a triathlon to be ridiculous, unfair and counterproductive. However, that cynicism was directed more at those in the wellness movement who seemed to be advocating for the use of diet, sleep and exercise as means of improving mental well-being rather than at the message itself.

I have always been dubious of the latest 'fads' that are proclaimed to be the panacea to mental well-being. While it might be OK to recommend the use of fish oils, mindfulness and meditation to those who are referred to as the 'worried well', they are not effective in the treatment of severe and enduring mental illnesses.

The whole concept of 'wellness' irks me, because it seems to be a very vague term that gets used by mental health entrepreneurs, some of whom can be guilty of selling snake oil to a vulnerable group of people.

An odd dynamic has evolved in the narrative of mental health, where there has been an attempt to move away from biological language when describing mental distress. But rather than this reducing the use of unhelpful 'illness' and 'disorder' labels, I fear it has inadvertently pathologised normal life problems, making them mental health problems. Initially, I supported the move away from the use of biological language to challenge the stigma that had become associated with mental health problems. Terms like 'mental illness' and 'mental disorder' were deemed outdated and stigma-inducing, and so a migration to more positive or palatable terms like 'wellness' and 'mental well-being' was the order of the day. However, in our attempts to make the conversation about mental health more accessible, have we perhaps lost a grasp of the core defining features of mental distress, which may be difficult to describe but are nonetheless important? Just because we don't use the term 'mental illness' does not mean we have eradicated mental disorders from existence.

These catch-all, non-distinct terms like 'mental health' and 'wellness' have been created to increase awareness, but they run the risk of diluting the meaning of these terms, which seems like exactly the situation they were trying to avoid. In contemporary language and media, we hear 'mental health' being described as a binary, single entity. It is something you 'have' or you 'don't have'. In reality, mental health is far more nuanced and complex than that. We don't talk about physical illness in this way, because we accept that it exists on a continuum of severity, so why do we believe it is OK to talk like this when it comes to describing mental health? Mental illnesses are complex, and they exist with a similar variation to physical health. There are mental health conditions that vary in a way similar to the way terminal cancer and the common cold vary, but these differences are often not recognised or acknowledged.

In an attempt not to pathologise *anything*, we have instead opened the door to self-diagnosis, which has pathologised *everything*. Some members of the 'wellness' industry have seized upon this window of opportunity to create lucrative initiatives within the 'wellness' space. I worry that these individuals benefit from the swell of self-diagnosis and can hijack people to spend their hard-earned money to treat conditions that they don't even have.

The wellness narrative runs the risk of oversimplifying mental distress. While it might seem comforting to imagine that all mental distress can be resolved by running a marathon, meditating every morning, or downloading a mindfulness app, it is at best naive and at worst exploitative. Many serious mental disorders require far more intensive support than this, and this message is not helpful to those who simply cannot 'walk it off'.

That said, when I began to realise that my reaction to the wellness messengers was far from the 4–7 zone, I began to read more of the research into the importance of diet, sleep and exercise in our mental health. The findings are indisputable. To establish balance and equilibrium in our lives, our bodies are the first place to start. There is no denying the symbiotic relationship between the body and the mind. Many of us will notice this two-way relationship between our bodies and our emotional lives. When we have an important event coming up that we are worried about, we can notice our sleeping patterns begin to be affected. Perhaps it's harder to fall asleep, or we keep waking up throughout the night. If we have a big job interview or an exam coming up, our anxiety can manifest in our bowels. We may experience physical cramps in our stomachs and have bouts of constipation and diarrhoea in the run-up to the event. If we have experienced a difficult life event like the loss of someone close to us, we can see that our bodies react by oversleeping or not sleeping, and we can feel exhausted all the time despite having had many hours of sleep.

Our emotional lives also have an impact on our diet. I can remember once when I was studying for a set of psychotherapy exams and I had left it very late to prepare for the Saturday morning exam. From the Tuesday of that week, I had to cram in as many hours of study as possible. I was pulling all-nighters and surviving only on multiple cups of coffee. I can remember my mother bringing me some toasted cheese sandwiches to try to get me to eat something, but the sight of them nearly made me sick. I had no appetite whatsoever from Tuesday to Saturday morning.

Once the three-hour exam was over – and thankfully I felt it had gone better than expected – the whole class gathered outside the exam hall to discuss the paper. While I stood around with my classmates, I couldn't concentrate on a word they were saying. I was so hungry. All I could think of was that there was a Burger King less than 300 metres away from where we were standing. I politely excused myself and went and ordered the biggest meal of my life. The point of this story is that my hunger and appetite were completely dependent on my emotional state. So long as the stress and anxiety about the exam were present, they completely eradicated my hunger, yet as soon as the exam was over and the anxiety had dissipated, my hunger returned with a vengeance.

So, with such an undeniable link between our emotional state and our diet, sleep and exercise in the form of physical symptoms, loss of appetite, and sleep and energy problems, it stands to reason that there must be a reverse dynamic at play too. It suggests that to maximise our emotional health, our sleep, appetite and exercise levels are fundamental places to start.

What is especially important when it comes to diet, sleep and exercise is that it does not have to be extreme. The biggest mistake people make when it comes to these dimensions of human behaviour is overcorrection. The temptation to slip into the 'new me' frame of mind is high, and many try to overextend their commitment to a healthy lifestyle, which proves unsustainable. Inevitably, after a short period, the unsustainability of these goals becomes clear and they give up. This leaves people with feelings of being 'a failure' or not enough, and as a result, their emotional health suffers as a consequence.

I will illustrate an idea of this overcorrection through the example of Adam.

ADAM

Adam is 47 years old, and he is married with two children. He works in a busy and stressful job as a salesperson, which involves a lot of driving and long hours. Adam recently attended his GP for an investigation into a series of repeated chest infections. While he was there, the doctor decided to do a series of physical tests. The test results revealed that Adam's blood pressure and cholesterol levels were higher than they should be, and he was overweight. The doctor strongly advised Adam that some lifestyle changes were needed if he was going to improve his current health status. Adam also suffered from low mood and intermittent bouts of anxiety and stress, but he did not mention this to the doctor, as he was embarrassed. He left the doctor's office and decided he needed to get to grips with his current lifestyle.

Adam went to a sports shop on the way home from the doctor's office and bought a new tracksuit and a pair of top-of-the-range runners. He downloaded the 'Couch to 10k' running app on his phone and pledged that he was finally going to do something about his lifestyle. He downloaded a 'carb-free' diet plan and bought all the ingredients that were recommended in the plan, deciding he was going to combine this plan with an intermittent fasting programme he had heard great things about. The following day was to be the start of his new regime. He was going to do it this time and he was not going to fail.

The first three days of his new regime started well. He was sticking to his carb-free diet plan, and he had been out running each day. He found the mornings OK, but he was getting very hungry by lunchtime and experiencing headaches. He also had two dizzy spells and had been unusually absent-minded when it came to some minor work tasks. Adam had not been running in over two years and he was experiencing pain in his lower legs, which Dr Google suggested was most likely a condition known as shin splints. He was not willing to let these issues derail his progress, as he was committed to doing this and getting it right.

Day 4 of Adam's regime was a Saturday, and it was his daughter's sixth birthday. There were lots of friends and family over for the party, and everyone was having a lovely time. There was lots of party food everywhere, and an especially delicious birthday cake. Adam began to pick at some of the treats in the bowls that were left out everywhere and also had some of his daughter's birthday cake because she was upset after he at first declined a slice. He promised he would go on an extra-long run later that evening to compensate for having the cake.

However, as the day wore on, Adam's shin splints got more painful. His plan to go for a run that evening had to be cancelled because his four-year-old son spiked a temperature and he had to go to a shop to find some medicine for him while his wife stayed with the children at home. When Adam eventually got back, it was too late to go for a run, and his legs were also very painful. He got annoyed with himself, as he had completely messed up his diet and exercise plan for the day. When he eventually got the children off to sleep and collapsed on the couch, exhausted, he decided that he deserved a beer. He opened a bottle of beer, and he and his wife enjoyed an episode of their favourite series with some beers and snacks.

The next day, Adam woke up deflated. He had failed already. He told himself that he had not even lasted a week and he was fooling himself if he thought he was going to be able to lose weight and get healthy. He reassessed the situation and estimated that the diet and exercise regime was too difficult and that he was a failure. The new tracksuit and runners were placed in the back of the wardrobe, and the carb-free ready meals passed their 'use by' date and were put in the bin. Adam had failed yet again, and not only had his diet, sleep and exercise habits not improved, but his low mood and anxiety had got worse. His self-worth was at an all-time low.

The problem with Adam's approach here was an overcorrection. He had flipped the dial too far in the other direction and attempted to go from 2/10 to 9/10 all at once. The goals he set himself were far too high, and therefore sustaining that level of change was always unlikely. Adam is not alone in this dynamic. It is something I see time and time again. It reflects our societal leanings towards the extreme. The popular narrative encourages us to go from 1–3 to 8–10 all the time. The adverts promise us six-pack abs in a matter of weeks or that we can get fit enough to run 10k in two weeks.

All of these slogans, while undoubtedly appealing, are grossly unrealistic, and create unattainable expectations. The promises of shortcuts and quick fixes are incredibly alluring, but the success rates are so small that they are rarely mentioned. There is normally an accompanying set of 'before' and 'after' images that are truly aspirational, with an accompanying caption saying something like 'This is Bob. Bob lost 2 stone in a week. You too can be like Bob.' This drive towards shortcuts and extreme interventions sets the expectation for success so narrow that most who attempt it will end up with feelings of failure. As unpopular as it may sound, slow and steady is the best formula for long-lasting change, yet no matter how well-worn that phrase is, or no matter how true it may be, the populist shortcut is far more appealing.

When Adam returned to therapy after his failed attempt at lifestyle change, we decided to readdress his goals with the 4–7 zone in mind.

APPLYING THE 4–7 ZONE TO DIET, SLEEP AND EXERCISE

Biology

Adam's biological markers had been established by the tests the GP had carried out. There was a need for him to reduce his cholesterol and lose some excess weight. These were the outcomes that were required for him to address the issues that had been raised. However, how these goals would be achieved was not established, and so Adam needed to work out a plan that would work around his current circumstances. The achievement of these goals was not set according to any timeline, and it was not a race against anyone other than Adam himself. By clarifying this, we immediately reduced some of the pressure Adam was feeling about achieving these goals.

Adam admitted to having a poor diet. As his work involved a lot of driving, he was a dashboard diner, which meant he normally bought a sandwich or a roll in the deli of a service station on his routes. This was normally accompanied by a packet of crisps and a fizzy drink. In the evenings, he would have dinner with his family, which was normally something that his children would eat, so it tended to not be made up of the healthiest of menus. Adam also remarked that his children were picky eaters, and when he was tasked with clearing off the table he would often find himself eating what they had left over instead of throwing it out, because he hated wasting food. Adam described the health of his diet as 2/10.

From a sleep perspective, Adam would describe working on his laptop for an hour after his children were asleep, and this brought him up to about 10.30 p.m. This was the time at which he would sit down to unwind and watch some Netflix. He said it was customary to have a beer and some snacks then, as he felt he deserved it after his long day. It would often be 1 a.m. before Adam got to bed, and he was up at 6.30 a.m. for work. Adam was getting on average 5.5 hours of sleep a night, and would rate the health of his sleep pattern as 2/10.

Adam used to be very sporty in his younger years. An avid rugby player, he played to quite a high level. He gave it up in his late twenties, as the number of injuries he was getting was affecting his ability to attend work. Also, when his children came along, he found that most of his evenings involved bring-ing them to their activities, limiting his own time to exercise. Adam's average activity every day is very limited because he is driving so much, and he would therefore rate his healthy exercise patterns as 1/10.

Psychology

Adam would describe his general outlook on life as poor. He has struggled in recent years to find any satisfaction in his life outside his role as an employee and a dad. This has affected his mood and self-worth, and in recent years Adam has struggled in both these areas. He rates his psychological health as 3/10.

Social

While Adam considers himself a very social person, most of his contact with other people occurs through his job. As someone who is on the road a lot, he spends lots of his time alone. He meets people throughout the week, but these are all work relationships, so the social element is very limited. Adam has a close relationship with his younger brother. His brother is successful, recently married and does not have any children. His brother's social life is considerably more active than Adam's. His brother regularly goes away to other cities for rugby games, but Adam is often unable to go because he is needed at home at weekends. Although Adam is very fond of his brother, he would admit to feeling envious of him at times. Adam would rate the health of his social relationships as 3/10.

Behaviour

As outlined above, Adam's behaviours are largely determined by his life circumstances. His poor sleep, exercise and dietary habits are formed around his lifestyle, and therefore behavioural change would need to accommodate these limitations. Some aspects of Adam's behaviours could benefit from minor tweaking, and that is the best place to focus any intervention. His previous attempt at behavioural change had not ended well, so he was feeling deflated about his chances of creating any mean-ingful change. As a result of his recent lack of success with a lifestyle change, Adam believed that when he feels better, he will do something different. Therefore, the first thing to address was this misconception, and to clarify that when you do something different, you will feel better.

Cognition

Adam's cognition was notably very negative. He had a very poor degree of self-worth and self-value, not helped by his recent per-ceived failure to instigate the lifestyle changes he had hoped for. He was also quite defeatist about his chances for change. He believed that his current lifestyle prevented him from initiating changes that would have any lasting effect, and he had resigned himself to the view that 'it is what it is'. However, we needed to challenge this mindset from the beginning, because belief is a cornerstone of success. The opposing view to 'it is what it is' is that 'if you do what you always did, you get what you always got'.

Emotions

Adam was not in a good place emotionally. The news from the GP had triggered a sense of his mortality, which led him to engage in a degree of rumination and negative emotion. He was experiencing his life choices as being 'wrong' and blaming himself for it. When we discussed this further, he reflected on the impact on his children of what he was doing. He felt bad for being a poor role model for lifestyle choices and was giving himself a hard time for not being healthier. He had even begun to think about scenarios where he would 'not be around for his children' if he didn't change his ways. I doubt it was the intention of the GP to trigger such a severe reaction in Adam, but the place he was in emotionally meant he heard it differently from what was perhaps intended.

MAKING CHANGES

Now let's use the 4–7 zone to illustrate how it can be used effectively to improve our diet, sleep and exercise.

Biology

Adam had rated his healthy choices in terms of diet, sleep and exercise as 2/10, 2/10 and 1/10 respectively. So, the goal would be to get those ratings up to a minimum of 4/10.

Diet

Some professionals might recommend that Adam should start to make his lunches for work the night before and provide complicated menus of hummus dips and celery sticks. But in reality, these interventions were not feasible for Adam in terms of the practicality of having time to prepare these lunches and, of course, the taste. We devised a plan that worked with Adam's current lifestyle. As the mainstays of Adam's diet were the deli roll with crisps and a fizzy drink, the only alteration we recommended was to replace the fizzy drink with flavoured water and perhaps change the type of crisps to a low-fat option. We also suggested that Adam not eat the leftovers from his children's dinner and perhaps have something other than a beer at night-time when he was watching TV. Adam achieved this almost immediately, and one month later rated his dietary health as 4/10.

Sleep

The goal for Adam was to limit himself to 10 p.m. when he was working on his laptop. Ensuring he was finished by 10 p.m. left a two-hour window to watch a movie if he wished and be in bed by midnight. This moved his sleeping hours from 5.5 hours a night to 6.5 hours and improved his sleeping pattern. This change took about a week to get used to, but one month later Adam rated his sleep pattern as 5/10.

Exercise

When we looked at Adam's schedule, we realised that his children had no activities on a Thursday evening. Coincidentally, a rugby club in the next town ran a social adults' touch rugby game on a Thursday night. As touch rugby is non-contact, the risk of injury was far less. The social aspect and competitive elements of the game appealed to Adam more than solo exercises like running the roads on his own did. This offered him an opportunity to move and engage in exercise for at least an hour a week. Adam also offered to help out with his daughter's football team. This meant that during the sessions he was no longer sitting in the car waiting for her to finish. Instead, he was out on the field setting up cones and drills and incorporating movement into his week. After one month, Adam rated his exercise and activity levels as 5/10.

Psychology

Adam had described his psychological health as 3/10 initially. He described having little sense of identity outside of his work and his family. His self-worth was low, and he felt like he was failing.

As Adam made the small changes to his lifestyle, he got to experience some 'quick wins'. The measurement of his success was not defined by the reading on the weighing scales; rather, it was measured by the effort he was making to make different decisions. These choices did not require a high commitment level, but the corrective emotional experience of being able to achieve – and more importantly sustain – a goal was a game changer for Adam. He would later admit that despite these changes being small, they had a big impact on his self-worth. His children would ask him when he returned from his touch rugby games, 'Did you win?' and, 'Did you have fun?' He described the fact that his children saw him role model and engage with a sport as significant to him. He had never been involved in anything like that since they were born, and he felt it was important for them to see sport as something that could be a lifelong hobby. After one month, Adam rated his psychological mindset as 6/10.

Social

Adam had little or no social contact outside of work. He felt that the people he met at work were people he 'had' to interact with, and although they were on the whole nice people, they weren't people he would choose to socialise with. He rated the health of his social network as 3/10. The major change here was that he felt he had found his tribe in the rugby club. These were people who shared similar interests, and he enjoyed the conversations with them. There was also a social night every few months where the group would meet up for drinks, and although this hadn't happened yet, Adam was looking forward to it. After one month, Adam rated his social life as 4/10.

Behaviour

The tweaks to Adam's behaviours were paying dividends for him. The improvements in his diet, sleep and exercise motivated him to make other behavioural changes. He bought some new clothes and paid more attention to his appearance and overall self-value. He was feeling energised by achieving these small goals, which provided him with the volition to make other changes in his life. The ripple effect of success is similar to the ripple effect of failure, and the positive experiences achieved through one behavioural change can often lead to another. One month after initiating these small changes, Adam rated his behavioural health as 6/10.

Cognition

Adam had initially been in a ruminative, negative thinking cycle. His failed attempt to change his lifestyle had left him feeling useless and ineffective. He had adopted a position of 'resignation' when it came to making any meaningful change in his life. Interestingly, it was the behavioural changes he made that seemed to impact his cognitive shift and not the other way around. So often we say that mindset determines behaviour, but neglect to acknowledge that behaviour can positively impact mindset. After an experience of failure, Adam needed to have a corrective emotional experience of success. That is why the small achievable goals were so important to this process. After one month, Adam rated his cognitive health as 6/10.

Emotions

Worryingly, Adam was in a dark emotional place. He had experienced his life as 'not enough'. His comparisons to his brother and his reflection on his lack of life achievements were affecting him in a very negative way. The visit to the doctor seemed to confirm many of the worries he had about himself. It was not that the doctor's concerns had upset him so much; they were merely a catalyst for Adam to think about a series of experiences he was having in his life that had caused him to feel like he was failing.

Adam was also quite alone in his emotional world. Not keen to share his worries or anxieties, he kept them to himself. This added to his sense of loneliness, and his lack of self-belief prohibited him from making the changes he needed so that he could begin to find some of his self-worth again. But the GP visit was a catalyst for positive change too. Sometimes, we have to be shaken out of ourselves a bit to realise that we need to make changes. Emotional upset can lumber on under the surface and sometimes a difficult life event can jump-start the process of decline or recovery. Initially, Adam's response triggered further decline, but later it was an important part of the changes that would impact his emotional life positively. After a month of cognitive, behavioural and social improvement, Adam rated his emotional health at 4/10.

CONCLUSION

What Adam's story tells us is that the knee-jerk 8–10 response is often the wrong option, despite its allure. Adam's keenness to flip the dial on his lifestyle and the seduction of the quick-fix brigade meant that what he attempted was an example of over-correction. He tried to change too much too quickly, and this inevitably failed. The message he was hearing was that extreme approaches were the way to go. Our obsession with gratification and speed has meant that many of us will fall into similar traps to Adam's. We want things to be vastly different in the shortest time possible, so fad diets and extreme exercise regimes are the order of the day. In reality, extreme changes only work in the smallest number of cases, and the risk of their increasing our feelings of failure is incredibly high.

The plan Adam adopted considered his baseline or starting point. It looked at what was possible, not what was optimal, and it looked at ensuring quick wins to optimise Adam's self-worth and maximise the chances of ongoing success and continued engagement. The reason why the 4–7 zone worked with Adam was because it focused on achieving fulfilling changes over gratifying dramatic results.

CHAPTER EIGHT

Technology

Technology has changed the landscape of our lives more than anything else in living memory. It has changed how we use money, book events, apply for jobs, communicate and relate. The evolution of technology has been impactful, but also rapid. It's hard to believe that in 2005 'Google' wasn't a verb and that the iPhone is only in its teenage years.

Our relationship with technology is also growing. In some ways, we are using technology more and more but also beginning to question it a little more. During its infancy, we had a romanticised relationship with technology. We were in awe of what it could do and we were unquestioning of its impact. However, as we have witnessed some of the more nefarious uses of technologies, such as internet scams, cyberbullying, vote manipulation and terrorist activities, we have grown to see it as a more nuanced phenomenon. This critical lens with which we see technology is a positive sign of our collective maturity when it comes to our relationship with technology, but it needs to be developed much further if we are to 'master' that relationship, using technology to better our life experiences instead of allowing our life experiences to be hijacked for the progression of technology.

There is no doubt that we have become more adept at using technological applications and platforms, such as Instagram, Twitter, TikTok and Snapchat, over the last decade. My mother is 77, and she watches Mass online and uses GIFs on WhatsApp. But our understanding of the depth of influence of these technologies on our mental lives is still far behind where it needs to be.

I completed my doctoral research on the area of the impact of online sharing. I was fascinated to find out what motivated us to share information online. I was also interested in the experience of online sharing and its impact on our mental well-being. What I realised in my study of the online world was that our relationship with technology was exactly that – a 'relationship'. It was something that was intertwined with our emotional lives and had far more influence on our sense of ourselves than we realised. In the same way as a copybook ceases being a copybook when we use it as a diary, so a phone ceases to be merely a phone when we invest and store our emotional secrets on it. Our phones are no longer a means of communicating with others; they are a means of communicating with ourselves. We store our diaries, calendars, pictures, notes and thoughts on the device. That is why we have such a strong reaction when we think we have lost our phone, or if someone else is using it and they begin to scroll. Our phones have become an extension of ourselves, and in many ways have become the storage facility for our intimate lives.

Despite a huge interest in the impact of technology on our mental and emotional lives, I am always struck by the lack of appetite for anything that will instigate any change in our relationship with technology or how we interact with it. There may be people who 'go off' social media on occasion, but a fundamental change in how we relate to technology is rare. Despite our awareness that this relationship comes at a cost to the other relationships in our lives, we continue to swipe, scroll and tap with mindless oblivion. But perhaps the thought of these 'fundamental changes' seems too big. I am concerned there is something about the messaging around this topic that is not getting through. The idea that we must engage in a 'tech detox' or travel to a remote retreat in the woods, with no Wi-Fi for six weeks, seems too much of an effort. However, perhaps there is a way of improving our relationship with technology that does not require us to act like monks and live our lives without a TV. Perhaps the answer to our relationship with technology is not about abstinence but about improved self-regulation.

When we think about the word regulation, many people assume that this requires some form of 'guideline' – that we need to adhere to some established level. This leads to the most common question I get asked when it comes to regulating technology use, which is a major one: 'How much screen time is enough or too much?' While there is no doubt that this is a reasonable question, it is the wrong question, and it is unanswerable for reasons I will now try to explain.

As technology usage becomes more pervasive and woven into the fabric of our lives, it has become a much more nuanced concept than this question reflects. It would be very convenient to be able to say, 'X is the optimal amount of time we should spend on screen per day. By adhering to this guideline, you will maximise the benefits of your technology use and minimise any negative impact on your mental well-being and daily functioning.' But this type of advice is neither available nor reliable, because we are all different people and have different relationships with technology, and this level of neatness and clarity is simply not possible.

Leaving it to others to regulate and control technology on our behalf is also naive. Technology is too big and too powerful to control, and attempts to regulate that space are becoming increasingly futile. There is also the issue of a lack of will – on the part of governments and technology companies – to make the online space safer, because regulating it may result in it losing its appeal, with a consequential reduction in potential profit, investment and jobs. The lack of regulation is the 'unique selling point' of internet technologies. While ideologists might foresee the development of a safer internet, my experience over the last decade tells me that this is extremely unlikely. Things like age verification or identity confirmation could have been integrated into internet technologies years ago. The reason they haven't been put in place is that anonymity is the main attraction of the space. If you plan to wait for the mandatory introduction of identity markers, then my guess is you're best to get comfortable, because you will be waiting a while. It is also important to realise that the developers of these innovative technologies are far more informed than those attempting to regulate them, and their motivations are fundamentally opposed to each other.

But that is not a reason for us to continue to blindly march off a cliff. We need to question this relationship at regular intervals and become a 'critical friend' of technology. Like with any relationship, the negative impact can be subtle, and we are often the last people to notice it.

Unlike other problematic relationships, like alcohol, food or gambling, there are very few visible or tangible markers of our relationship with technology. Overuse of alcohol may be noticeable because of the number of hangovers we experience, overuse of food may be visible through our expanding waistline, and overuse of gambling may be noticed in our dwindling bank balance. The same cannot be said about technology. Once you pay your monthly bill, your Wi-Fi is unlimited, so there is no obvious monetary cost. We rarely experience any form of abstinence because our phones are rarely turned off. And there are no obvious physical symptoms because we are 'always on'. It is only when we cannot access our addictive activity that we recognise our dependence on it, so many of us are completely unaware of what kind of relationship we have with technology at all. In many ways it is similar to alcohol becoming available like tap water: we would all be largely unaware of how dependent on alcohol we would be and would possibly carry on in blissful ignorance.

But the use of technology is not without its consequences. Although the consequences may not be visible in terms of an observable symptom, that does not mean they are not subtly impacting our well-being.

THE IMPACT OF TECHNOLOGY ON MENTAL WELL-BEING

In Chapter Three I referred to the words of Winston Churchill when he said that we shape our buildings and they then shape us. This sentiment rings true when it comes to technology. The technological infrastructure has had lasting effects on how we function. The advent of camera phones has made the action of getting photographs developed obsolete. Instead of photographs being special moments captured in time, they have become a digital record of everyday events. The capacity to store information in our phones has removed the need to remember things like phone numbers. Smart payments have almost completely done away with the use of cash in society. The roles of the travel agency and the printed newspaper are becoming less a part of our society, and the trip to the record store to buy the latest album from your favourite artist is a thing of the past for most people.

I don't mention these things as a traditionalist who laments the ways of the past. I am merely explaining how the evolution of technology has changed our behaviours. Some years ago, the idea of being on your phone playing a video game while you were sitting on the toilet would have been perceived as incredibly odd, but now it has become a normative behaviour, and sitting in a waiting room for 30 minutes with one other person and not making any eye contact at any point would have been interpreted as bizarre. Now, it is completely normal. I am reminded of a funny comment a friend of mine made some time ago where he said, 'I saw this guy in Starbucks today, no iPhone, no laptop, no tablet. Just sitting there drinking coffee. Like a psychopath.' This joke is a commentary on how things have changed and how the new normal has become normal and the old normal has become deviant.

That's not to say all technological advances are bad; they are not. But there are some aspects of human behaviour that technology is bypassing that are worrisome. There is a fear that with the advent of technological options, we run the risk of 'throwing the baby out with the bathwater'.

I am reminded of a personal experience where I was in a shop paying for a newspaper and a coffee. When I went to tap my card, the cashier informed me that the 'tap wasn't working'. She proceeded to apologise, which I can only assume was because my face displayed some degree of disgruntlement. It was like I had said, 'What? Do you mean I have to press four digits and an enter button? This is ridiculous!' In reality, only a few months before I had pressed four digits without any problem. Why had it suddenly become an issue?

The reality is that the easier things become, the harder the easy things appear. This is why the evolution of technology has impacted our mental and emotional experiences. It is not that things have got harder; it is because our expectations of things have got higher. Remember: Reality – Expectation = Happiness. With such expectations of speed, convenience and gratification, we have become intolerant of boredom, waiting and fulfilment. This upward drive of expectation has impacted our experience and expectation of happiness and enough. The concept of enough is central to our mental well-being and is perhaps a core determinant of it, so if technology is negatively impacting our concept of enough, that's a big deal.

It is not just the speed, convenience and gratification of technology that are negatively impacting our concept of enough. There is also the role of social media and its creation of the 'hypercomparative culture'. As mentioned before, social media shows the highlight reels of people's lives, and therefore negative comparison is inevitable if we don't acknowledge this. However, as human beings, we have a natural inclination to focus on our deficits, and this is problematic.

For example, if you received a report card with eight A grades and one F grade, your attention would be immediately drawn to the F grade. That's just how our brains are wired, so when it comes to social media we tend to forget about the factors that manipulate other people's highlight reels and instead become concerned about why our experiences aren't as good as theirs. Another personal example of this might be when we are sitting at home on a Friday night watching TV and we feel content. We then turn to social media and see our friends out in a fancy restaurant eating a lovely meal, and we experience envy. All of a sudden, our experience of contentment is no longer enough, and we become unhappy or unfulfilled. The reality is that we invite those intrusions into our lives. By opening the social media site, we invite comparison, and this impacts our sense of contentment and enough, and ultimately our emotional state. The problem, therefore, is not our reality, but our expectation of reality.

This is why technology can impact our well-being. It inflates our expectations of the world and ourselves in a way that leaves us feeling disgruntled and experiencing discontent. We were not built emotionally to be able to deal with such a degree of social comparison. With the volume of information-sharing available, we simply become victims of information overload. The content is overwhelming and therefore our capacity to establish and maintain balance becomes grossly impacted. In a world that celebrates extremes, the moderate becomes more and more difficult to establish.

So how do we defend ourselves against the tirade of expectation and comparison? Well, first we need to reconfigure our relationship with technology and establish a means of regaining some control over our choices, and the 4–7 zone is an ideal method for beginning and maintaining that process.

RECONFIGURING OUR RELATIONSHIP WITH TECHNOLOGY

One of the most common metrics we use when describing our relationship with technology is 'screen time'. Although often associated with children's use of technology, it has a wider significance in the adult population too. We see the time spent on our devices as the indicator of whether we have a problem or not. But this metric tells us very little when it comes to mental well-being, because it is not simply the time spent on technology that is important, but much more the impact of online activity on our sense of ourselves and the world.

For example, I could spend an hour on YouTube watching a guitar tutorial and trying to learn to play a particular song. I would consider this a good use of my time. I am learning a new skill and relaxing, and when it is over I might feel like I have accomplished something good and feel positive about myself. Alternatively, I might spend another hour looking through my ex-girlfriend's Instagram profile and feel utterly lousy about myself because I see how much more she has moved on from our break-up than I have. Afterwards, I feel preoccupied and sad. By using the screen-time metric, it will just say that I spent an hour on each activity and take no consideration of the impact of that hour on my mental and emotional well-being. We therefore need to move away from a *time spent* focus and move towards a *time well spent* focus. By adjusting how we measure online activity, we become more aware of the cost of online engagement as well as the potential benefits.

A useful analogy is to consider technology in a similar way to food. Certain foods are better for us than others, and a varied, balanced diet is what is optimal, but what this consists of will vary from person to person. The same goes for technology. Some online activities are better for us than others, and it is not about never engaging with them, but merely incorporating them into a varied, balanced technological diet. We don't judge the health of our diet by the amount of time we spend at the kitchen table or by how long it takes us to eat our food. What we strive for is a healthy, balanced diet of fruit, vegetables and other nutrients and the odd bar of chocolate or trip to McDonald's. Nobody would suggest that anybody should expect to have a life without ice cream, but likewise, we wouldn't encourage ice cream for breakfast, lunch and dinner either. The difficulty with our technological diet is that the activities that are not helping us to feel better are harder to identify. We may not notice how scrolling through social media sites, comparing our homes to those of interior design influencers or getting sucked down a rabbit hole of Twitter spats is eroding our souls.

Differentiating between time spent online that encourages learning, fun or interaction and time spent on activities that compromise our self-worth can be difficult, and that is why it is worth investing time into being more conscious of the net result of these activities. Not all people are the same. Just as some individuals are aware of their sweet tooth and can stop reaching for the treat cupboard, even enjoying an apple from time to time, some people are effective self-regulators and will know when they need to disconnect. It is those who require a lock to be put on the treat cupboard and who are poor self-regulators of technology that require more attention and support. If we learn to approach technology in a similar way to the way in which we approach food, we will be more informed about the choices we make around how we spend our online time. A balanced diet of technology uses screens for work assignments combined with time for less productive activities such as watching videos of cats on skateboards.

The key is that we need to tailor our technology diet to our lives. Those who are more likely to make sensible choices and self-regulate may require far less surveillance than those who have difficulty with self-regulation. This characteristic is related to our vulnerability. Therefore, we need to move the emphasis from regulating content to regulating desire. That's not to suggest that continued efforts to regulate harmful content – such as sex abuse, hate speeches or racism – should not continue, but a parallel process to improve our media literacy and educate users to regulate their desire needs to occur alongside it. Even if you were to clean up the internet and remove all harmful content, you would still have people who would spend nine hours on TikTok dances. This is not illegal or inappropriate, but it's just not a good use of their time. So even if we regulate content, we still have the issue of regulating human desire.

The work in improving our relationships with technology needs to focus on humans, not machines. The 'user' is the key variable, and to create good technological relationships we need to support users to become critical consumers of technology and make choices that work for them rather than for the tech companies.

The 4–7 zone will help us achieve that.

THE 4–7 ZONE WITH TECHNOLOGY

Looking at the numbers, it seems pretty clear that many people have problematic relationships with technology characterised by excess. Many of us may be shocked to hear that our usage is so pervasive that many of the self-reporting statistics are gross underestimates of how much people refer to their devices over a typical 24-hour period. When asked to estimate our screen-time usage, a large majority estimated 40 per cent less than the actual figure. However, despite this underestimation of our usage, most studies reveal that most people are aware they use their phones too much but find it difficult to stop.

As humans, we think of ourselves as rational beings who are very capable of making our own decisions and exercising full control over our own choices. However, we all have vulnerabilities that can be exploited by outside influences. One of the areas of influence that can exploit our vulnerabilities is the design of technology.

Tristan Harris previously worked as a product ethicist for Google, and in later years made a 'hunter-turned-gamekeeper' move when he openly revealed how his role in Google was to develop persuasive technologies to maximise users' time on screen. This involved a team of people being employed to study human behaviour and develop ways in which human psychology could be manipulated to captivate the attention of users in order to maximise time on screen. Things like notifications appearing in the colour red and even the sounds that accompany these notifications were picked because it was believed that these were the most effective ways of capturing users' attention and hyping up the importance of checking what the notification is about.

Harris made the comparison to the design of casino-based slot machines when it came to designing social media platforms so they could hack into our psychology and trick us into spending more time on screen than we hoped to. Harris described how we live in an 'attention economy', and our attention is the currency for the platforms' business models. The more attention they can command, the greater the market share of attention they control and the more they can charge for advertising and data. In the pursuit of captivating our attention, all the social media and online companies have engineered ways to habitually alter our everyday behaviour and keep our brains engaged in their agenda.

So even if we don't recognise or admit that we have an issue with our use of technology, there is merit in exploring this relationship to protect ourselves from being manipulated into spending time, money and energy on agendas that are not our own but are decided by large tech companies.

I will use the example of the case of Julie to illustrate how the 4–7 zone can be used to keep tabs on our relationship with technology.

JULIE

Julie is a 32-year-old woman who lives in a one-bedroom city centre apartment. She works in marketing and finance at a large multinational company. Three years ago, during the global pandemic, Julie had to work from home. Last year, the company offered its employees the option of returning to the office or continuing to work from home. Julie considered this at the time, and although there were some perceived benefits in returning to the office, the drawback of having to get on a crowded bus every day and queue for her coffee won out, and Julie opted to continue working from home.

Julie has one brother who is married and living in Germany, and both her parents moved to a small town in Spain when they retired. Julie visits them twice a year and calls her mother twice a week. Julie has some friends that she went to school with, but many of them have children and busy work lives, so they have lost touch in recent years and rarely meet up anymore.

Julie's social connections consist mostly of her friends within her online gaming community. As an avid gamer, Julie likes to play strategy games on her PC as a way of relaxing. She has met several people through the chat rooms and gaming communities and Julie enjoys their company. Many of these people live abroad and Julie has never met them in person, but she still maintains strong relationships with them online. Most of her friends in the gaming community have similar interests to Julie and she enjoys their company, but the major issue is that they are functioning in different time zones, so the conversations tend to be late into the night or early morning.

Julie also makes her own jewellery. She has a small business, selling her creations on Instagram. She is a member of several dating sites, but rarely goes on actual dates, as she finds them very anxiety provoking.

Let's use the six criteria for a mental health check to examine Julie's current relationship with technology.

Biology

Although technology use does not directly impact our biological functioning, it can very easily disrupt our routines and lead to poor biological self-care. In Julie's case, her technology use disrupts her sleep, diet and activity levels.

Sleep

Julie sleeps an average of four hours per night. As she and her colleague Geoff work from home, they have the freedom to work independently. But their roles are very intertwined, and so they often need to work on projects together. Geoff has two small pre-school children, so his days are very busy. Geoff says he works better at night-time because the children are asleep. Therefore, his main hours of work tend to be from 9 p.m. to 1 a.m. This means that Julie often has to log on to her laptop at these times to see what Geoff has been doing and to answer any queries.

The main advantage of working from home is the flexibility that it offers, so for people like Geoff, it means he can work late into the night and leave time during the day to be with his children. However, this flexibility does not help Julie, as she is often quieter during the day and gets busier late at night when she would prefer to be unwinding and getting ready for bed. Working from home offers great freedom, but with great freedom comes the need for stronger boundaries. While remote working is fantastic and means we can work from anywhere, it also means we can work from everywhere, and we therefore need to be self-disciplined around limiting our work.

Julie would not consider herself assertive in her work role and ends up working the hours that suit Geoff's schedule instead of her own. Furthermore, as Julie's gaming friends are in different time zones, any live interaction with them often occurs in the early morning, because that is when most of her peers are online. Regularly, Julie is only getting into bed at 2 a.m. and is setting her alarm on her phone for 5 a.m. to get up and chat with her online friends. This lack of sleep is having an impact on Julie's mental well-being, as she describes feeling tired a lot of the time.

Diet

Julie rarely cooks meals, because she sees it as a lot of hassle for one person. The mainstays of her diet are cereal and toasted sandwiches, which are handy to prepare and don't require having to wash any pots or pans afterwards. Julie is not overweight, so she doesn't pay much attention to her diet, but her consumption of starchy carbohydrates and sugars and the absence of any fruit or vegetables in her diet must, we can assume, negatively impact her energy levels.

Exercise

In terms of activity, Julie is almost completely inactive. Except for infrequent trips to the local takeaway coffee dock or the shop, she partakes in little or no activity. Again, as she does not struggle with her weight, Julie does not believe activity or exercise to be necessary. However, she does worry when she is completely breathless taking the stairs to her apartment. To manage this, she now takes the lift instead.

From a biological perspective, Julie is a 2/10 in terms of diet, sleep and activity, and she has been this way for some time.

Psychology

From a psychological perspective, Julie would have always considered herself anxious, especially in social situations. Despite being charismatic and likeable, she always struggled with self-doubt. Even as a teenager she would often come away from a casual conversation and ruminate over what she had said or not said during the encounter. This was an exhausting process, and over time she would just say less and less in conversations and actively avoid going to places where informal social encounters were expected. Julie believes that technology changed her life for the better.

The advent of text-mediated conversations suited Julie. She liked the fact that she could take her time to consider and control what she was about to say before she said it. She much preferred this method of communication to live conversations. Julie would actively avoid engaging in any conversations and would always opt for text or email communication instead. This is what she loved about her job. Weeks would often go by when Julie would not have to speak to anyone, and all communication was via email. While Julie preferred this controlled method of communication, it wasn't without its challenges. She would often agonise over the wording she was using in emails. She would draft and reread and redraft different versions because they were too inflammatory or too breezy. She would often spend over 30 minutes editing a four-line email until she believed she had got the tone 'just right'.

This was also evident in her social relationships. Julie much preferred communicating with her online peers, as a lot of that was through the 'chat' function using typed responses. More recently, she has engaged in verbal exchanges on her headset, but she feels OK about this because the conversation is primarily about the game she is playing at the time, and the pleasantries of social conversation are not required. In terms of Julie's dating life, when she matches with someone, she will often chat with them for a few weeks, but when the other person suggests they might meet up in person, Julie usually withdraws from the conversation.

Julie's self-worth is very much bound up in her jewellery-making business. Although she considers it a hobby, she invests a lot of time in this activity, not only in the creation of the pieces but in the marketing of them. Julie always gets very anxious when she finishes a piece of jewellery, as she must then post images of it online to see if people like it. When a piece receives positive feedback, Julie feels euphoric. This acknowledgement and validation are really important to her and make her feel high about herself. However, when her pieces receive negative feedback, she can become devastated and really upset. This can cause her to become down about herself, and she has often vowed to never make anything else again. However, she then finds herself dismantling that piece of jewellery, no matter how much she likes it herself, and starting a new piece. Julie can spend hours browsing through other creators' Instagram pages and always feels deflated that her work is not as good as theirs. This leads to the belief that she is not as good as they are.

Julie's psychological state is similar to her physical/biological one. She has created a life of avoidance, and because there are no glaring 'symptoms', she believes she is doing OK. However, the latent or hidden effects of her avoidance are there, and so she has become fearful of confronting them and they are festering beneath the surface. Julie only realises how unfit she is when she has to use the stairs in her apartment block, so she chooses to use the lift. She only realises the extent of her social anxiety when she is asked to go on a physical date, so she disengages. Her habit of outsourcing her self-worth to a mob of online commentators is also problematic, and her willingness to disassemble her jewellery creations on the back of some negative feedback is also concerning in relation to her sense of herself. Julie's psychological state is a 3/10, despite her not being completely aware of it.

Social

Even though Julie has an active social life and social network online, her offline social world is non-existent. While she may be grateful for the evolution of online technology that has facilitated her ability to be social in a way that bypasses her social anxiety, this method of interaction will do nothing to address or confront her fears of face-to-face interaction. Online communication is convenient and suitable for those with social anxieties, but it does not do anything to help them instigate any change to do anything about their anxieties. If anything, the continued avoidance of the anxiety-provoking situation only serves to make it even more feared. Also, text-mediated communication like email and text messaging offers the user a sense of control, but in reality this is an *illusion* of control. Despite feeling reassured by the ability to edit and delete messages before we send them, the space for rumination over those few lines of typed text is endless. So rather than reducing our anxieties, the capacity to control communication in this way may indeed be adding to it.

Given the current limitations to Julie's offline social world and the ongoing anxieties that she carries, I would think her current social functioning is around 2/10.

Behaviour

The obvious fundamental behaviours we could look at surround Julie's sleep, diet and exercise. Her basic pillars of well-being are nowhere near optimal. These are quick fixes that with some minor adjustments could offer a significant improvement in her ability to take on other challenges. The social avoidance habits that she has developed are becoming more ingrained and auto-mated at this point and are going to be more difficult to address.

Julie's willingness to remove her jewellery creations because they receive one negative comment is also problematic. This action confirms that the opinion of 'the other' holds more weight than her own views and opinions. By removing and disassembling her creations, she is compromising her self-worth and allowing others to determine her value, which is having an ongoing impact on her low self-belief. Perhaps by leaving the item up and gathering more comprehensive feedback, Julie might realise that her creation appeals to a far greater number of people than the number of people who are not keen on it. This could act as a corrective emotional experience and help her to persevere with her own beliefs.

Julie's current behavioural functioning is 3/10.

Cognition

Julie's thinking style appears to be dominated by a lens of anxiety. She sees aspects of her life through the lens of threat. This fear of things going wrong dominates her actions, so she has created a life for herself that avoids situations she finds challenging. However, avoiding the circumstances we find challenging will never challenge the negative thoughts we have about ourselves. For Julie to create different cognitive pathways, she will need to create different life experiences. This will mean that combining the act of challenging her negative thinking about herself and challenging the comfort of avoidance will offer Julie the evidence she needs to create different beliefs about herself and her ability.

The habits of negative rumination and forensic analysis of all of her social encounters are core aspects of Julie's difficulties. She may believe this forensic analysis of real-life conversations will allow her to better prepare for future encounters, but in reality they only serve to spiral into a pool of negativity and confirm her negative beliefs about herself.

Currently, Julie's cognitive functioning is a 2/10 and her rumination levels are 9/10.

Emotions

Julie is surviving life. This means she is doing what she can to get by and is looking for as many short-term solutions as she can to navigate her life and relationships. However, these short-term solutions are also technological shortcuts. They offer her temporary relief from emotional discomfort, but they create longer-term avoidance issues which are more problematic. The link between Julie's technological relationship and her emotional life is not immediately obvious, but deeper exploration reveals that it is having a significant impact.

Much like alcohol, food or illicit substances, technology can be used as a means of coping with or escaping uncomfortable realities. In Julie's case, I believed technology was her means of avoiding social relationships that troubled her. Immersion in the virtual world made engagement with the offline world surplus to requirements. However, this avoidance, like alcohol or food, can create bigger long-term problems. When we escape the uncomfortable, a reliant relationship on that escape activity can emerge, and when we rely on something so heavily, dependence is inevitable.

The other subtle impact of technology in Julie's story is the interaction between her emotional self-worth and her online activity. The way in which her self-value is bound up in the feedback and validation of her Instagram commentators is important. As soon as we offer up our self-value to the feedback of what is essentially a mob, we are vulnerable. Julie's emotional vulnerability is evident in how much this feedback means to her. Some might see her posting her jewellery creations as bragging or narcissistic, when in reality it is the very opposite. Julie is not 'announcing herself' on Instagram; she is trying to 'find herself'. This is a dangerous game to play. We all see ourselves through the eyes of the other. The feedback we receive is important, and don't believe anyone who says it is not.

But what is more important is our ability to apportion value to those people who are offering us that feedback, and this is the tricky bit. There is truth in the saying that you should never accept criticism from someone you wouldn't go to for advice. The online world has allowed everyone to have an opinion and a voice, and the mistake many of us make is allowing all those opinions to hold weight. Some people in our lives deserve our attention and they have earned it. Others have not. If we allow people the capacity to impact us emotionally without their having earned that right, then we leave ourselves open to emotional compromise. This is what has developed in Julie's case, and it is hurting her emotional well-being. Overall, I would consider Julie's emotional functioning as 3/10.

It was this emotional state that spurred Julie to contact me. She opted for online therapy sessions over Zoom, and as she told me about her story and experiences, the aspects of her life that were causing her emotional pain became clear. The following is how we implemented the 4–7 zone to help Julie to manage her emotional life a little better.

MAKING CHANGES

After an honest discussion with Julie, we introduced the rocks, pebbles and sand metaphor that I referred to in Chapter Five in relation to Jim and his work–life balance.

Julie identified that close and intimate relationships were her rocks, her online gaming friends and her jewellery business were her pebbles, and her work performance and pleasing people were her sand. This revealed that the way Julie *wanted to* prioritise her life and how she *was* prioritising her life were opposites. In light of this revelation, we began to work on instigating change and implementing the 4–7 zone.

The first aspect we needed to look at was how Julie could improve her biological and behavioural scores. We first identified the need for improvements in her sleeping patterns, discussing the variables that were at play that were disrupting her sleep and which of these dynamics were movable. Julie immediately identified working late to accommodate Geoff's timetable and having to get up early to navigate her friends' time zones.

Julie assumed that I was going to suggest that she reduce the time she spent chatting with her overseas peers online. I went with a different approach, however. Given that Julie's self-worth was so low, I was keen for her to continue to spend time doing the things that made her feel good about herself and to spend less time on the things that had the opposite effect. Rather than suggest she have less social contact, I was keen that she would maintain as much social interaction as possible, even if it was limited to online chats.

We explored why Julie was willing to work around Geoff's schedule and why he was not willing to work around hers. Julie explained that because Geoff had children, his needs trumped hers. I challenged this and asked why she assumed this to be so. Geoff had chosen to have a family and had opted for remote working. Therefore, there was as much of an onus on him to be flexible as there was on Julie. Julie was fearful this was going to cause conflict between her and Geoff and was reluctant to communicate it to him. I explained that this was her first effort to own her value and that sometimes that process can be initially uncomfortable. Julie's agreeableness is part of her anxiety and needed to be challenged for her to overcome it.

There can be no change without discomfort, and I offered Julie support with that discomfort should it arise. Together, we scripted an email to Geoff, politely explaining that Julie would not be available to address any live issues after 7 p.m. most evenings and would not be accessing her emails from 7 p.m. to 7 a.m. most days. She suggested that if Geoff had a query that required a response, she would do her best to get to it first thing the following day, but that he should not expect a response before then. To Julie's surprise, Geoff replied stating that he never expected her to respond in real time and that Julie should feel under no pressure to do so. He was aware that his schedule was inconvenient and said he would endeavour to work more traditional office hours in future.

It seemed that Julie's expectations of herself were the issue here. There was no need for her to be online while Geoff was working, but her anxiety meant that she would 'prefer' to be available in case she missed out on something. Sometimes anxiety prefers us to be hypervigilant instead of blissfully ignorant.

Julie now needed to tolerate the uncertainty of leaving her work tasks to the morning and resist the urge to check. I encouraged her to instead try to get to bed at an earlier time so that she would feel rested for her early start at 5.30 a.m. to chat with her online friends. At first, Julie struggled with this change. She said that although she was in bed by midnight, she struggled to fall asleep any earlier. After about a week of persisting with getting to bed earlier and not checking her work laptop, Julie's sleep improved. She was noticing that she was feeling more refreshed during the day and her energy levels had improved.

When we looked at Julie's diet, we considered the idea of her having at least one 'proper meal' per day. To overcome the hassle of making meals every day, Julie came up with the idea of making two meals on a Sunday evening and keeping extra portions in the fridge to use again. She began to cook a pasta bake and a vegetable curry on Sunday afternoons, and this served as her dinners during the week. She continued with her toasted cheese sandwiches for lunch.

In terms of her activity, we suggested that Julie could walk to a coffee shop that wasn't the nearest to her, but was near the coastline, once a day. We suggested that Julie put aside 30 minutes for her lunch every day, make herself go and get the coffee and walk one length of the pier. Julie committed to doing this and reported that her energy levels in the afternoon were better than they had been previously and that her 3 p.m. slumps were less frequent or severe. She still opted for the lift, though, but we both agreed to let that slide.

In terms of her psychological and cognitive habits, we explored the 'why' of Julie's low self-worth. Julie explained how this dated back to her adolescence. At school, she was never one of the 'cool people', and she explained how her fashion sense was 'a bit out there'. She also explained how her body developed more quickly than her peers' bodies and how she was teased a lot about this. Julie used to shop in thrift shops and liked to adjust the clothes she bought to make them more contemporary. The other teenagers in her school did not appreciate this ingenuity and creativity, and she was teased for being a 'weirdo' and 'poor'.

Julie explained how this experience made her untrusting of people. She had some close friends in school who one day turned on her and joined the 'cool people', and she was left alone. Any attempts she made to integrate into the mainstream group resulted in her being excluded. She joked that these experiences 'left a scar', and she began to believe that if so many people did not want to be around her, there must be something wrong with her.

This became a core belief, and Julie went through the rest of her life feeling that she was a burden on people and that anyone who engaged with her was merely humouring her. She had a core belief that 'people let you down'. This cognitive lens of presumed betrayal meant that she feared closeness. She desired closeness more than anything, but what she wanted the most was also what she feared the most, so she opted to avoid feelings of vulnerability by not starting any close relationships with anyone. She explained that she felt she was attracted to online relationships because they made her feel less vulnerable. But she firmly believed that if any of her online gaming friends or the people she chatted to on the dating apps met her in person, they would no longer like her.

Extensive therapeutic work began when we tried to explore and challenge these long-held beliefs. We examined the long-term impact of her experiences of bullying and exclusion on the lens through which she saw her relationships and herself. We needed to begin to challenge the automatic negative thinking that Julie had about herself.

The first method of challenging this view of herself was through her Instagram posts. Julie had a habit of allowing other people to determine the value of her work. She had a high sensitivity to criticism, which was likely to have been a result of her peers teasing her fashion choices as a teenager. The task set for Julie was to try to tolerate the negative comments and not allow them to get to her. We discussed the subjectivity of art and how one person's rubbish can be another person's treasure.

I also encouraged Julie to reframe the criticism and try to react proportionately to its value. We used the example of how, if you were walking down the street and someone who was drunk shouted something at you, you wouldn't take it personally, whereas if someone you knew and respected said the same thing to you, you would be upset. The key was to place a value on the commentary of others and respond accordingly – the mantra of 'those who matter don't mind and those who mind don't matter'. Julie tested this out and reposted an image of a piece of jewellery she had received some negative comments about previously. I asked her to leave it up for a minimum of two weeks and see what the overall themes of comments revealed. She did this, and the breakdown revealed that over 90 per cent of the comments were positive and the other 10 per cent were not actually negative about her piece, but represented random venting from troll accounts. This process allowed Julie to respond in the 4–7 zone and not react in the 8–10 zone.

Finally, we needed to work on Julie's emotional state. Once she reframed her cognitive habits and understood why she had avoided social situations as a result of her past experiences, we needed to bring this progress of thinking into the realm of doing. With improvements in her sleep, diet and activity (they were now all 4/10) and healthier thinking processes that were no longer afflicted by negative automatic thoughts (currently 4/10), the final goal was an improvement in her emotional well-being. This would be the most difficult, because it would involve having to tolerate some emotional vulnerability.

The task was for Julie to bring some of her online relationships into the offline world and to try to manage her social anxiety. There was one young man whom Julie had been chatting with who had asked her to go for a coffee. Julie, with much encouragement, eventually agreed. Despite high levels of anxiety, she went to meet him for coffee. She said he was pleasant and nice, and both were able to chat about things for almost an hour. Julie had a fake escape route planned if the date were to go badly or if her anxiety were to become unmanageable. She survived the date and managed to not overanalyse or ruminate about the encounter too much after it was over. She went on another cinema date the following week and enjoyed this too. It turned out the man in question was looking for something more serious than Julie was, so they amicably parted ways after the cinema date.

Julie was really happy that she had managed to survive two high-level social engagements and had enjoyed them. This corrective emotional experience was a great boost to her self-worth. It led to her reconnecting with two of her cousins whom she had drifted apart from socially over the last year, and they made plans to go out again. Julie had finally managed to broaden her social world into the offline world, and she was very proud of herself. She maintained her links with her online peers, but was happy that she didn't have to rely on them completely for her social outlets.

Julie's reliance on technology had been 9/10 at the beginning of therapy and her offline social world had been 1/10. Her biological self-care and behavioural lifestyle habits were 2/10 and her social anxiety about meeting people in person was 8/10. Julie's tendency to overthink and ruminate was 9/10 and her ability to be dismissive of comments by people whom she did not value was 2/10. After making small adjustments to her sleep pattern, diet and activity levels, and clarifying her availability to her colleagues, she brought these numbers into the 4-7 zone. By understanding the reasons for her insecurity in social situations and her fear of being betrayed, abandoned or ridiculed, she was able to begin to challenge these core beliefs about herself and commit to beginning to shape some new core beliefs about herself. All of this permitted her to make brave behavioural steps, which included tolerating the risk of negative online feedback and surviving the anticipatory anxiety of going on an actual in-person date.

Julie was someone who believed that when she felt better, she would do something different, when in reality it was only when she did something different that she was finally able to feel better.

CHAPTER NINE
Parenting

Most of my career has focused on trying to understand the world through the eyes of a child. As a mental health nurse and psychotherapist, I have worked with children and families for over 25 years. One of the most important aspects of that job is trying to understand what different life experiences feel like from the perspective of a child and how childhood behaviour might be understood through these experiences.

Over the last 25 years, there have been some presentations that have remained fairly constant. The incidence of childhood depression, self-harm, eating disorders and ADHD (attention deficit hyperactivity disorder) have presented at a reliable level. However, the one presentation that has skyrocketed in the past 10 years is childhood anxiety. I have never in my whole career witnessed so many anxious children – and more anxious parents. Our culture has become riddled with anxiety and stress, and the impact of that is being experienced by families. There are many theories as to why this is happening, including academic pressure or poor coping strategies, but the main culprits for the surge of anxious children seem to be technology and parenting.

There is no doubt that technology has changed the landscape of family life. It has altered how we work, communicate and function. Technology has brought with it a dynamic of information overload, and this has happened to both parents and children. One of the impacts of technological evolution is the emergence of the hypercomparative culture referred to already, where we are overinformed about the highlight reels of other people's lives. With our expectations rising higher and higher, this has had a significant impact on the role of parents. 'Competitive parenting' has emerged, and now we need to demonstrate our parenting effectiveness and share it with the world. Our children have always been seen as an extension of ourselves, so their successes and failures are intrinsically reflective of our parenting skill set.

Parenting has changed in recent years. Over the past decade, we have seen a parenting movement emerge where there are multiple books, podcasts and column inches dedicated to how to parent. It used to be said that there is no 'how to' book when it comes to parenting, whereas now there are almost too many 'how to' books, leaving parents anxious and confused. Parenting is something that many couples are desperate to 'get right'. This automatically heaps more pressure on parents not to get it wrong. As a result, parents are reading books, doing parenting courses and seeking professional advice on how best to 'parent' their children. But what has happened is that our children have now become commodities that reflect our investment, and this has been an unhelpful association because of the overwhelming pressure that has come with this trend. It is my opinion that this dynamic has contributed significantly to most of the parenting problems that currently exist.

A colleague of mine once asked me what I thought were the main problems facing children's mental health, and I replied that they were 'expectations, stress and pressure, information overload, reduced opportunities to practise autonomous decision-making and too many adult-led activities in their lives'. In response to this list, my colleague commented that these 'are all adult-created problems', and they were right. Most of the issues and challenges to children's mental well-being are created by adults. When we consider the issues in children's sports, where some clubs have had to put in place 'silent sideline' rules and referees at underage games have been assaulted, it is clear that these are not issues with the children; they are issues with the adults. This suggests an issue of adult overinvolvement, and these are symptoms of some of the problems with modern-day parenting.

What I have also learned over the two-and-a-half decades of working with families is that parenting is transgenerational. That is, it carries through from generation to generation. In some cases, young couples will choose to try to emulate their parents' style of parenting, as they felt it was a good template because they 'turned out OK'. Others will vow to parent their children in a completely different way from their parents, because they believe their experience growing up was suboptimal and left them with a certain degree of emotional baggage. Whatever the response, there is little doubt that how we experienced being parented has influenced how we parent our own children.

Another rationale that parents sometimes have is to provide their children with all the opportunities they 'never had' themselves. This can often result in parents dedicating a significant amount of time and effort to developing their children's skill sets and experiences. This can include access to impressive educational opportunities or supporting their engagement in sports, music and other interests. Sometimes parents feel that they were held back from fulfilling their potential and therefore vow to not allow this to happen to their children. While this seems a very noble endeavour, it can sometimes put families under a significant financial strain, or else a dynamic emerges where parents are living out their own lives vicariously through their children.

All of these influences can distort our experience of parenting as much as they can enhance it. We need to be aware of our own parenting biases to avoid making extreme decisions when it comes to parenting our children. One of the most common topics that parents disagree on is how to parent their children, and it is not unusual for the arrival of a child to bring some of the core differences that exist in couples to the surface. Many of us are attracted to people who possess opposite qualities to our own. However, when these differences emerge in the form of differing approaches to parenting children, tension can emerge.

Many people find getting married easier than becoming parents. In many cases, one parent may be more relaxed and passive when it comes to rules, discipline and expectations compared with the other parent, and when these styles collide, confusion and frustration can ensue. This can be difficult to manage.

When it comes to parenting, nothing is more important than balance and equilibrium. Like most things related to mental well-being, the moderate route tends to be the most effective. That is why the 4–7 zone is so effective when considering the best approach to parenting.

USING THE 4–7 ZONE IN PARENTING

Most of the questions I get from parents surround a concern about a particular behaviour, and are followed by the query 'Is this normal?' The behaviour involved tends to be something a child is doing in response to feelings of anxiety. They can include a child who has a fear of dying or of other people dying, a child who is perceived to be 'behind' in terms of their developmental milestones, a teenager who is restricting their diet or exercising to the extreme or a child who is presenting with some behaviour management problems in school. While a significant percentage of these concerns are valid and would raise some red flags in my mind about needing some intervention, others are decidedly normal. Childhood and adolescence are challenging life phases, and some difficulties are to be expected.

A common example is that at around the ages of 7 to 11 a child will go through a phase of fearing death or worrying that someone close to them will die. This usually occurs at night-time when they are due to go to sleep, and can be a worry for parents. However, this fear is normal and is related to the child coming to terms with 'permanency'. At this age, children are reaching the 'age of reason' and can consider the concept of consequences, and they are trying to figure out which life experiences are temporary and changeable and which are permanent and irreversible.

Many children can struggle to comprehend the concept that things change forever, and so they seek reassurance from this worry by talking about concepts like death. In most cases, this is a phase that passes once the child comes to terms with the concept and moves on. However, parents can understandably become anxious and wonder if their child's worry is a sign that something more sinister or pathological is going on. In situations like this, parents tend to have some predictable responses. Some perceive the child's behaviour as a display of severe anxiety symptoms and frantically look for the child to see a therapist straight away. Others choose to try to ignore the child's anxieties and dismiss them as being 'silly', or get annoyed when the child brings up the topic of death.

The reality is that both of these responses are in the 8–10 and 1–3 zones and are not advisable. I have found that children can provoke extreme responses in parents. Because of the closeness of the relationship between child and parent, we can sometimes be hypervigilant and see things that aren't there, and at other times we can be so close to the child that we miss things that to others are glaringly obvious.

The distortion caused by the parent–child relationship can be fascinating to observe. The hypervigilant parent who is seeking weekly therapy sessions because their child is expressing some anxious feelings is displaying an 8–10 response, as they are overestimating the seriousness of the behaviour. On the other hand, the parent who dismisses the child's worries by getting annoyed and telling them to 'stop talking about such silly things' is displaying a 1–3 response, as they are shutting down the channels for the child to express their worries.

Both of these responses could have negative consequences. If the hypervigilant parent was able to source a therapist for their child, it could make the child feel that their worries are more serious than they are. The child's anxiety could rise, and they could feel that there is something seriously wrong, worrying even more as a consequence. It is important to note that seeking professional psychological intervention is not always the best option, especially for normative developmental challenges, as it can create more anxiety for the child than is necessary. As for the parent who dismisses the child's worries about death by stating that they are being 'silly' or gets angry when the child brings up their worries, they may be making the situation worse too. If the child feels that they cannot discuss their worries, they will not be able to process them and come to terms with them. Instead, they are given a message that they are 'wrong' to worry, which can be interpreted as there being something 'wrong' with them. This can lead to the child internalising their worries and allowing them to fester, thereby making the feelings of anxiety worse.

The 4–7 zone response in this instance is optimal. In a 4–7 response, you hear what the child has to say about their worries. You allow them time to express their worries, but try not to embellish them, because this can result in a cycle of rumination. Reassure the child honestly by explaining that death is a part of life, but that in most cases it does not happen until people are much older and that everyone in their own life is fit and healthy, so that while it is important to be aware of it, it is nothing they need to worry about right now.

Another important aspect of the 4–7 zone is that we must allow children to venture into the 8–10 and 1–3 zones from time to time. This is normal. What is important is that as parents we try not to have them stay in those zones for too long. In the case of reassuring a child about the concept of permanency and death, this may require several conversations for the child to process it. None of us learns French verbs by hearing them once, and so children need time to have these conversations repeated until they are satisfied and can move on. If we as parents role model a 4–7 approach to our children's anxieties, there is a greater chance of them returning to the 4–7 zone in terms of their own management of their worries. In parenting, we must accept that our actions have an impact on subsequent actions for our children, and therefore our reactions or responses are crucial in determining the improvement or deterioration of our children's experiences.

A similar dynamic can emerge when parents consider their child's performance and behaviour in school. When it is brought to the attention of parents that a child is struggling in school, some parents can again have a hypersensitive response and assume that there is something very serious going on. I have had many parents approach me in search of professional support because their child is struggling a little in school in terms of behaviour or academics. This is an example of an 8–10 response.

However, children are like popcorn kernels: despite the same conditions, they don't all pop at once, and later in the process it is impossible to tell which ones popped first. What I mean is that developmental milestones are sometimes seen as targets to be reached, when in reality some children are just a little slower to mature, especially socially and emotionally, and what they need is a little more scaffolding or support in class, not a battery of assessments and tests. Especially in the early years of school, they may just need the adults in the room to be more patient.

On the other hand, there are parents who, despite numerous reports from teachers of glaring gaps in behaviour or academics, are reluctant to acknowledge that there are any issues and are reticent about referring their child for any support. This is an example of a 1–3 response. In these circumstances, the measured, thoughtful response is optimal.

Take on board the reports from the teacher, but integrate the approach and temperament of the teacher too. Some teachers are intolerant of any behaviour that involves non-conformity or non-compliance, and this needs to be considered when deciding on what to do.

Giving something a little time to settle is always worthwhile, and never underestimate the value of 'keeping an eye' on something. Time can resolve many childhood issues, and often a slight change to the level of support or the approach to the child can make all the difference. If the problems persist, despite time and supportive interventions, then there is a definite benefit to acting, but jumping in prematurely with an 8–10 reaction, or dismissing all concerns and delaying any action with a 1–3 reaction, is not helpful.

THE 4–7 RULE IN ACTION

Rather than take one case example, I am going to describe how parents can use the 4–7 zone to guide their parenting decisions over a range of different scenarios and age groups. I will use the six criteria for a mental health check as a template for where these parenting dilemmas can emerge.

Biology

When it comes to our children's physical well-being, every parent will want their child to be healthy. Most assume that this is achieved through a well-balanced diet, reasonable activity levels and the right amount of sleep. This can be challenging at times, especially when children are constantly tempted by sugary junk food, own their own handheld devices or gaming consoles and don't enjoy organised sports. No parent sets out to compromise a child's health through obesity, poor diet or inactivity, but this can evolve quickly, and it becomes a challenge to manage these habits without risking giving your child a complex about their weight and shape.

There is also the other end of the spectrum, where parents become obsessed with providing their child with a wholesome diet and insist on all food being made from scratch, with no processed foods or trips to McDonald's. Some children are subscribed to far too many sports, which can lead them to develop repetitive strain injuries before their bodies have fully developed.

A friend of mine is a physiotherapist and he told me that he has never seen so many young children presenting for treatment of sports injuries. When I was a child, I didn't even know what a physiotherapist was, nor was I ever aware of any of my childhood peers needing to attend a physiotherapist. My friend's theory is that children's exercise now is sporadic and overly structured compared with years ago. Children's physical activity tends to be limited to training sessions and matches, and many are not naturally active in between these times. This might explain how children are entering into sometimes intense and rigorous exercise 'cold', when strains and pulled muscles are more likely to occur. There is also growing evidence that children are less able than previous generations to engage in fundamental movements like jumping and skipping, which is also contributing to their injury difficulties. To summarise, my friend said he has met children 'who can sprint and kick a ball but haven't got the co-ordination to master a sweeping brush'.

This is an indication of the issues with children's diet and activity. Some parents are far too lenient with sugary foods and treats, where their regulation of their children's diet is in the 1–3 zone, while others are bordering on obsessive in their approach, no 'bad foods' are kept in the house at all, and a celery stick with hummus is seen as a treat.

The reality is that these extreme approaches to children's diet and exercise are both problematic. How we help children create good relationships between food, exercise and body image is through a moderate approach. There is no such thing as 'good' and 'bad' food. There are only good and bad 'amounts' of food. It can be as counterproductive to have a strict food culture in a home as it would be to have an overly lenient one. The same moderate approach is applicable to childhood obesity.

All children should be active, and movement is an essential aspect of their well-being. But training at multiple sports five nights a week with two matches every weekend is not healthy either. Making all activities and movement about competition is a mistake we are making with our children. Since adults have become overly involved in children's sports, the fun element of activity has dropped, and the intensity and commitment levels have increased. Competitive environments are not for every child, and sometimes they can serve to deter children from remaining active rather than encourage them. Competitive sporting environments suit the child or teenager who loves to win and has a competitive attitude. These are the children who were probably going to be active anyway. However, the avenues are very limited for a child who doesn't share that competitive edge or who does not want to commit to twice weekly training and matches at the weekend.

I meet lots of teenagers who have retired from their sport, or in worse cases have 'been retired from sport', because they were deemed not good enough or not competitive enough. But most teenagers will say the reason they left sport was that 'it wasn't fun anymore'. This overly serious aspect of children's sports is again a result of the adults, not the children. Adult coaches and organisers are the ones who are responsible for setting the tone of sports clubs, and I lament the fact that many have completely missed the point of what social childhood sport is all about. Parents play a role in this too. I have heard of children leaving a sport because the coaching team was too serious and intense. The coaching approach was in the 8–10 zone of competitiveness. I have also heard of parents taking their child out of a sporting club because they felt the coaching attitude wasn't serious enough and they feared that what they saw as a lax 1–3 zone intensity was not going to allow their child to achieve their potential.

This leads me to the next aspect of parenting where the 4–7 zone needs to be considered: the realm of psychology.

Psychology

The lens through which a child sees the world is heavily influenced by their family. The family's culture creates a template for value systems that children will adopt or reject. We must not underestimate how, as parents, we have a significant role in the relationships children form with peers and themselves. The most important relationship any of us will form in our lives is the relationship we form with ourselves, but we see ourselves through the eyes of the other, which means that how we receive feedback from those around us shapes the feedback we provide for ourselves. As parents, we need to be aware that the voice that a child hears from us is similar to the voice they hear in their own heads.

I believe that the three most important aspects of a child that will determine their mental well-being are their self-worth, self-belief and self-value. These aspects of 'the self' play a significant role in a child's relationship with themselves and in turn in their relationship with the world around them. There is a misunderstanding about these concepts where people often refer to 'self-esteem', which I believe is an important concept to clarify for many parents. At a talk in a school some years ago, a parent asked me a brilliant question. She asked, 'How do you strike the balance of getting your child to be assertive and have a good opinion of themselves, without turning them into a brat?' The honesty of this question gets to the heart of the self-esteem issue. We all want our children to believe in and stand up for themselves, but is there a risk of overdoing that narrative to the point that they naively overestimate their ability and set themselves up for disappointment when real life kicks in, or even worse, they become self-obsessed or self-centred and show little compassion towards the needs of others?

For this reason, the 4–7 zone is important.

Good self-esteem is not the same as an overly inflated ego. Good self-worth is having a good relationship with yourself that is based on self-belief and accuracy. This includes an awareness and acceptance of our limitations. Along the way, some aspects of developing good self-worth got muddled and we thought it meant telling our children that they are 'special' and destined for special things. All parents think their child or children are special, and they are. They are special *to you*. However, not everyone can be special. The exclusivity of 'specialness' is kind of a core part of its meaning. If everyone is special, then no one is special. So, children need to realise that they are very special to their family and friends, but that this does not necessarily translate to the wider world. And that's OK.

Good self-worth should mean that we don't need to be special at all things; rather, we accept ourselves for who we are and embrace our skills, strengths and limitations. However, it is a little different in childhood. The progression through childhood involves a paced introduction to the harshness of life. If a six-year-old child says they want to be a professional footballer like Ronaldo or Messi when they grow up, it is perfectly acceptable to agree with that fantasy, despite having a distinct belief that it will not transpire. However, if the same child is 19 years old and beginning to find their way in the adult world, and they still believe that they are going to be like Ronaldo or Messi even though they cannot nail down a place on their local soccer team, then that fantasy may need to be confronted and the bubble of delusion may need to be burst.

This is the process of maturity – moving from the 'imaginary' phase of childhood to the 'real' phase of adulthood. What is crucially important about this developmental progression is the pace of the introduction of reality. If it is too quick, the child is made to feel overwhelmed, defeated and ineffective, but if it is too slow, the child will be vulnerable to being disappointed, excluded or manipulated. This is why the pace of 'reality orientation' needs to be within the 4–7 zone.

If a child is prematurely exposed to content or experiences that are beyond their emotional or social maturity, they risk being traumatised or missing out on important developmental steps. For example, a child of a parent with an addiction may need to protect their younger siblings from their parent's behaviour. They are burdened with responsibilities they are too young to cope with, and this is an introduction to reality within the 8–10 zone. Alternatively, a child may be overly sheltered from the adversities of life. Their homework is always supervised and corrected by parents before submission, they are consistently told that their successes are exceptional and their failures the fault of others, and they are overrewarded for mediocre achievements. This could create a sense of entitlement, presumption and naivety. The pace of this introduction to reality is in the 1–3 zone. In both of these examples, the feedback these children are receiving from the world is not preparing them to be ready to cope with the demands of adulthood.

Nurturing a sense of self in the 4–7 zone means gradually introducing the child to the realities of life at a pace they can manage. Ideally, they would have experiences of authentic joy or achievement and moderate levels of failure or disappointment. The experiences of failure and disappointment must be within the range of 'surmountable stress'. Surmountable stress is a level of discomfort that engages the child in activating their coping strategies to manage and get through the adverse experience. This might include doing poorly on a test, a falling out with friends or being dropped from a sports team. These types of challenges are not to be bypassed or avoided; instead, they are to be navigated through with support and guidance. The 4–7 zone approach to parenting would recommend that parents do not leave a child alone with their struggles, as this would be a 1–3 zone response; nor should parents try to deny the presence of these challenges through overprotection, as this would be an 8–10 zone response. By surviving adverse experiences, children get to road-test their coping strategies, and although difficult at the time, these experiences serve to nurture the child's self-belief, because they now have an experience of negotiating adversity that they can take into the next inevitable challenging life event.

Finally, self-worth is an internal phenomenon, not an external one. Self-worth comes from our relationship with ourselves and thus is intrapersonal and nurtured by internal variables. Parents do not always understand this, but believe a child's self-worth is nurtured by awards, grades and accolades, which are external variables. When a child is feeling low or anxious, parents attempt to make them feel better by reminding them of what they are good at. 'Don't be sad. You are a great soccer player.' 'Don't worry. You are really clever at maths.' Despite these comments being well-intended, they communicate to the child that these are the metrics by which we value their worth. This inflates the value of the external variable and leaves the child needing to perform in these areas in order to feel enough.

The 4–7 zone of parenting would suggest that the external variable is at times gratifying, but that it is not fulfilling. The internal variables are far more sustainable aspects of self-worth. Our internal variables are not what we are good *at*; they are what is good *about us*. Internal variables include kindness, bravery, loyalty, purpose, courage and strength. These are the pillars of self-worth, and the external variables are pillars of self-confidence. The 4–7 parent places much more value on the internal variables than on the external ones, and this serves to create a much more robust sense of self in the child. Some examples of this approach would be to comment on the child's effort rather than the outcome of their task – for example, making a comment like 'You have put a lot of time into that drawing. That's really impressive', or, 'I notice you seem to be giving your all to your basketball training at the moment. That's really good.' The focus on outcome over effort is a habit we need to break. When a child comes home from a sporting activity, we tend to ask, 'Did you win?' and, 'Did you score?' Instead, we might ask, 'Did you enjoy it?' and, 'Did you try your best?', which are much more validating questions and allow the child to see where our priorities as parents really are.

Social

There are two social aspects to parenting. One is the social development of your child, and the second is the role a child plays in your social relationships.

In terms of supporting your child to navigate social relationships, there is a developmental context to this process. As parents, we have a fairly 'hands-on' role in our children's friendships in the early years. The concept of 'play dates' has meant that in many ways we can oversee and guide the friendships our children have. When they are older and more independent, this becomes much more difficult, as it is very much left to the young person to make friendship choices.

The way in which we prepare children to make those choices is therefore important. The best approach is to try to instil a value system around what friends are and what they should be. Over the years, I have witnessed how the child's relationship with themselves is crucial to this dynamic. How we feel about ourselves is what we project outwards into the world; therefore, an overinflated view of our own importance can result in behaviours that are self-serving or dismissive of others. On the other hand, if we have a poor relationship with ourselves, we will be overly accepting of poor treatment of ourselves by others and not assert our own value enough. This can lead to us being walked over, which means that people treat us poorly and we allow it. Sometimes if we place too much value on being accepted or 'fitting in', we can have these experiences too. A child who is desperate to be part of the desired clique can sometimes abandon their own standards in order to take part.

If we want our children to have the best chance of a healthy social world, then the work begins with establishing a strong sense of themselves and a belief in their own value that is accurate, authentic and espouses the value systems of inclusivity and compassion towards others. This might sound really difficult, but with the guidance of the 4–7 zone, it is possible.

When developing a child's self-belief, some parents can over-convey a sense of the child's own importance. A child who is repeatedly told they are 'the best' and constantly compared positively with others must also be told about their social responsibility to other people. It is absolutely fine that a child is a great soccer player, once they can be aware of and empathetic towards others who are not. It is fine that your child is a whizz at maths, once they are compassionate towards others who struggle in that area. It might be great to know that your child is one of the most popular children in their class, but that must be accompanied by an awareness of the more vulnerable children there, and your child must show compassion towards them.

These are examples of the external variables (maths, sport, popularity) and the internal variables (kindness, compassion, empathy). We must be careful not to overdevelop the external variables at the cost of the internal ones. When considering the social development of our children, we need to aim at a balance of 4–7 in all of these areas. If a child's skill set is in the 8–10 zone, it is crucial that their compassion and awareness of others are not down in the 1–3 zone. Like Spider-man's uncle famously said, 'With great power comes great responsibility', and this is an integral aspect of the 4–7 zone.

But what if your child is not the superstar of the soccer team or the child prodigy mathematician? What do you do then? Well, if your child is neither of these things, take solace in the fact that he is like 80 per cent of other children in the world. Most people are not brilliant or terrible. Most people are average, and that's how things are supposed to be – it's kind of how the concept of average is defined. There has been a recent drive to demonise average, which is putting our children under incredible stress to be exceptional, and I believe this is contributing to the crisis of childhood anxiety that we have been experiencing. (I will discuss that in more detail in subsequent chapters.)

You may think that I am favouring the idea that children place more meaning on the internal variables over the external ones, and while I do believe the internal variables are more nourishing to our self-worth, they are not without their complications either if children are overinvested in them. Some children can overvalue the internal variables of compassion and empathy. There are many children I have seen who become overly affected or involved in the lives of others. Those with a more anxious temperament can lie awake at night worrying about the welfare of others, the climate crisis or a distressing news story. While we want our children to develop a social consciousness and compassion for the plight of those who are less fortunate, that too needs to be within the 4–7 zone.

Because children struggle to master emotional regulation, they can overdo their application of empathy, and this results in their anxieties being in the 8–10 zone. In these cases, it is best for parents to try to coach the child to navigate the social world in a way that doesn't overwhelm them and leave them disproportionately upset. An example of how we can strike a balance here is by using the 4–7 zone philosophy and perhaps mentioning a topic to a child without labouring the point. For children who have a psychological antenna for worry, perhaps the emphasis needs to be on the hopeful aspects of a story. If there is a tragedy hitting the news headlines, perhaps less detail about the awfulness of the event and more emphasis on the compassionate response of the local community would be advisable. In terms of climate anxiety, we can alert our children to the climate change issue, but focus more on what can be done to help rather than on the grimness of the outlook in future years. As a parent, if you are faced with two polarised options, it is often best to ignore both and aim for a middle-ground response to your child's needs.

The focus of a parent's energy should be on protecting and maintaining a child's self-worth and being proactive in managing any circumstance that compromises that. If we believe that how we feel about ourselves determines how we express ourselves in the world and in turn how the world responds to us, it is crucial that children have a good idea of what is acceptable in their lives and what is not. This involves every child setting a conceptual bar in their head that indicates the spectrum of experiences and guides them towards what they should expect and accept and what they need to call out and not tolerate.

This conceptual bar is based on the philosophy of self-respect and tolerance. Children will experience social challenges throughout their lives and, as parents, we need to provide them with a guide as to what is OK and what is not OK. For example, childhood friends will argue and fall out over things – that is a given. When these incidents occur, it is important to provide a context for the child to understand how to perceive them and how to respond to them. For example, if two small children fall out over a game or who played with whom, this is a 4–7 problem. It is normative, and as parents, we need to coach our children to have a 4–7 response to the incident. This process teaches children that there will be things that will happen that we will have to manage, and it promotes their ability to prioritise and react proportionately. Your daughter might come home and tell you about the disagreement she had with her friend, and it is up to you to role model how best she can manage it. If the parent overreacts and says, 'I am going to tell your teacher what happened and

I am going to have a word with the girl's parents', this is an 8–10 reaction that can have a negative impact on the child's self-worth. It suggests that the other girl is wrong and nobody should ever challenge you, thereby making the simple, everyday situation into a big deal and creating anxiety in the child. On the other hand, if the parent reacts by telling the child to 'get a grip and just find other friends', without listening to what the child has to say or hearing their upset, this is a 1–3 reaction. This communicates to the child that their experiences and upset don't matter, and this has a negative impact on their self-value or self-worth.

The 4–7 response is what is required at this point. Listen to what the child has to say and acknowledge their upset. Then try to get them to see the situation for the other girl and see if there are any factors that might explain why she acted the way she did and whether there were reasons for her response. Then try to introduce some context and perspective into the conversation by suggesting that this falling out is likely to resolve in time, and suggest ways in which the child can respond, react or manage the situation. If the situation escalates and the child is being bullied or excluded, then an escalation in the response may be necessary, but for the most part, these micro stresses are wonderful learning opportunities that teach a child how to regulate their emotions and responses to better serve their management of social situations.

An important clarification for children to be aware of is the difference between 'fitting in' and 'belonging'. If a child is desperate to be part of a group of children in their class, they may be willing to be mistreated or dismissed in order to be accepted. This reflects the fact that their conceptual bar of self-respect is too low. This again reflects a poor relationship with themselves that may mean their self-worth is in the 1–3 zone. In this instance, the parent needs to address this issue promptly and get that up into the 4–7 zone.

This can be achieved by finding a space for the child to be introduced to their 'tribe', and by this I mean like-minded people who accept them and validate them. This is often an extra-curricular environment away from school like scouts, drama classes or being with extended family or cousins. It is as important to provide the child with positive emotional experiences as it is to try to manage or reduce their negative experiences. Many parents spend years trying to manage a child's experience of exclusion in school without spending time finding a space where they feel included. For the child, being accepted may cause their self-worth to temporarily jump into the 8–10 zone, but the ongoing inability to assert themselves will have an eroding effect on their self-worth over time. One of the most common phrases I have heard from teenagers I have treated in recent years (and which I have referred to earlier in this book) is 'I spent all my life being who other people wanted me to be, and I forgot to be myself.' This is an indictment that children and young people are not being authentic. They are prioritising fitting in over belonging. This is where, as parents, we need to help children prioritise and own their own values.

The key to helping a child to navigate their social world is to keep their dial of self-worth and their interactions in their social world in the 4–7 zone. This is best served by providing them with an understanding of the difference between the internal and external variables and supporting them to keep those within the 4–7 zone.

The second aspect of the social world of parenting is the role your children play in a parent's social relationships. When we become parents, it can be an all-consuming experience. Inevitably, aspects of our pre-parenting lives will have to be sacrificed. However, it is important that some degree of balance is maintained during this process. It is very easy for our social world to be built around our children. Our weekends are spent going from sports pitches to swimming pools and waiting on the sidelines or galleries. The other parents can become our social network. While this is not problematic in itself, if we have no other aspects to our social world our children's activities can become disproportionately central to it.

We are hearing more and more incidents of parental over-involvement in children's activities – parents encroaching on pitches in underage games and referees being abused by vocal parents on the sidelines. This for me is a result of the dynamic where our children's lives have become disproportionately dominant in our own adult lives. People ask me why a parent would become so angry or upset about an under-10 football game, and one of the explanations is that they have nothing else to be obsessed about and are venting all of their energies through their child's activities. It is crucially important, but admittedly very difficult, to maintain your own social world outside of your child's activities. It serves to dilute the intensity of these occasions and offers a more balanced approach. The same can be said of adults involved in coaching children's activities. Often after a loss on a Saturday morning, the children have recovered by the afternoon and are out playing, whereas the adult coach is the one ruminating over what went wrong in the game.

The 4–7 zone informs how parents need to manage their social world in terms of their children's activities. If you are a parent who has never seen your child play a match and never attended one, your child may feel invalidated and forgotten about. This is a 1–3 zone approach. However, if you are attending every game and training session and repeatedly being asked by the coaches and referees to tone down your sideline behaviour, this suggests your approach is in the 8–10 zone and needs to be addressed. Being a parent is only a part of your identity, and if that is proportionate and within the 4–7 zone, you will be doing fine.

Behaviour

Behaviour is a key aspect of childhood and there is a very good explanation for why this is so. Where language fails, behaviour takes over. When we feel something that no words can capture, we act out. This might be seen in the frustration of kicking a piece of Lego that we just stepped on in our bare feet, or the exasperation of the exclamation, 'Aaarrraaagh!' These actions and this word capture the limitations of language. Thankfully, these incidents are few and far between for adults, because we have mastered a comprehensive collection of words to accurately describe most situations. The most difficult language to master is the language of emotions, because sometimes our feelings are beyond words, and it is then that we act out or behave in a way that conveys the intensity of that emotion.

Now consider the same dynamic in children or adolescents. They have a much more limited collection of words to describe emotion, and therefore they must resort to behaviour to communicate how they feel. Take the toddler, for example, and how the phenomenon of the 'Terrible Twos' is something many of us are familiar with. The Terrible Twos phase is characterised by a collection of severe and extreme behaviours – the defiance of rules, the catastrophic reactions to what are seemingly the most innocuous of events, and the rapid-cycling mood changes from devastation to euphoria. This is because the toddler spends almost no time in the 4–7 zone. Their complete emotional and behavioural zone is 1/2/3/8/9/10. This is because they cannot express in language how they feel, and behaviour is the most effective way of getting their point across. As parents, we play a role in this because we react and respond more promptly to behaviours, and the more challenging the behaviour, the more promptly we respond. So, the primary role of the parent is to coach a child to be less 1–3 or 8–10 and more 4–7 in their behaviours.

We regulate all the time as parents. We regulate our children's sleep, appetite and behaviour, and by doing this we are inadvertently trying to coach them to regulate their emotions. This is best done when the regulation of behaviour is accompanied by the provision of language. Curbing behaviours without providing language is only partially effective. For example, if a toddler is going to put their hand on a hot radiator, we might say, 'Ah, ah, ah, no.' However, this behavioural instruction is without context or meaning. Compare this with 'Ah, ah, ah, no. If you touch that it will hurt your hand' (maybe mimicking a sore hand with an accompanying 'ouch'). This provides meaning and context to the behavioural instruction. Children need a 'why' as well as a 'what' when it comes to commands, and we often overlook this.

What we need to understand as parents of younger children is that the extreme 1–3 and 8–10 behaviours of younger children are normative and to be expected. Despite what the brochure told you about parenting and the image of the elegant mother in the rocking chair gazing into the infant's eyes, parenting is hard. The reason it is hard is because you are tasked with trying to regulate and rationalise with a human being who is utterly irrational and unregulated, and that's OK. That's the way they are supposed to be. Their ability to think about their feelings and experiences is underdeveloped, so they communicate through behaviour. As adults, we feel, we think and we do. Toddlers, children and even teenagers have big feelings and very little capacity to think about these feelings, and as a result they must rely heavily on behaviour or 'doing' as a means of communication. As a parent, you are going to be interacting with little people who have feelings in the 8–10 zone and the capacity to think and rationalise in the 1–3 zone, and it's going to be challenging as a result. Therefore, managing your expectations of parenthood and children's behaviour is crucially important for how you experience and manage parenting.

Don't be swayed by the parents at the crèche who claim their child sleeps 12 hours every night, or never creates a problem and is being considered for 'advanced education' because their numeracy is so good. Those parents are struggling too – 80 per cent of parents struggle with the task of parenting and the other 20 per cent lie about it. I am kidding, but by its very nature parenting small children is difficult, and so it should be. We tend to believe when our child has challenging behaviour that we are doing something wrong or that there is something wrong with them. While in rare cases some of that might be true, in most cases we feel that way not because our reality is a problem but because our expectation of parenting and child behaviour is a problem. Many of the parenting queries I get are not because there is something that a child is doing that is out of the ordinary; it is often the case that what the parent is expecting is not in line with the child's developmental level.

Here is my attempt to dispel the myths about children and young people's behaviour:

- Most small children and infants will struggle to sleep at some time or another.
- Toddlers are not capable of being reasoned with, so if you are trying that tactic, that's why it's not working.
- Children and teenagers will test boundaries; it is their way of learning and exploring their world, and it's not a sign of a problem.
- Sibling rivalry and inter-sibling fights and arguments are normal. They exist in an attention economy and are in an arms race for your attention, and this is going to cause conflict from time to time.
- Your timetable is of no concern to children, and nor should it be. Your toddler will not master toilet training because you want them to have it sorted before you go back to work after maternity leave on the second child. They will do it when they are ready.
- Teenagers will become more distant from you as they get older. It is not about you; it is their way of becoming independent. They need to do it to practise coping without you.

Despite childhood and teenage behaviour in the 1–3 or 8–10 zones not being abnormal, the most important aspect of this developmental stage is how long this behaviour continues. The defiance of toddlerhood should pass. The truculent teenager should become less so over time and the anxious child who is lying awake at night worrying about the future of the world should not be doing this indefinitely. Veering into 1–3 and 8–10 is not the problem, but if this continues for longer than it should, then there could be an issue. If your toddler has a tantrum in the supermarket because you refuse to buy them a pack of chocolate buttons, that's to be expected. However, if they are 19 years old and still have the same reaction, then an intervention may be required. Remember, behavioural dysregulation is not the problem, but the inability to regulate behaviour over time may well be.

A relatable example of this might be when your four-year-old child comes into your bedroom at night and says they have had a nightmare and they believe there is a monster under their bed. The most natural response might be to say, 'Jump in here then,' and allow them into your bed – then everyone gets a night's sleep. However, the next night, the child returns telling you they are worried about the monster under the bed again. The response here is crucial. If the duvet is flung over and the child takes their place in your bed, then you may be creating a longer-term problem. If your child is 11 and has spent the past 7 years in your bed, then changing that habit is going to be an issue.

The other problem with this response is that you might believe you are communicating the message that 'I love you and I care about you' when you invite the child into your bed – and you are. However, what you are also communicating is 'There is a monster under your bed and you need to be in here with us.' This promotes a feeling in the child that they need to be in your bed, as they are not able to sleep independently. A more cumbersome response is to take the child back into their room, check under the bed, reassure them that there are no monsters and encourage them to sleep independently. While doing this whole rigmarole with a four-year-old in the middle of the night might seem like a pain, this is the 4–7 response. If you adopt the 1–3 response and allow them to stay in your bed again, you can only imagine the months of late nights and the 8–10 response that will be needed when they are 11 years old and you are trying to get them back into their own room when they haven't slept independently for 7 years.

Sometimes our responses to children's behaviour come with the best of intentions, but it is always useful to think about the middle ground. If any of your responses to children's behaviour are overly passive or dismissive, they are likely to be in the 1–3 zone and problematic. Similarly, if your responses to your children's behaviour are extreme, intense and emotively charged, chances are they are in the 8–10 zone and equally problematic. If faced with two options that are polar opposites when it comes to parenting decisions, consider the middle ground option. If your teenage son is struggling with maths and your choices are to get him to leave school and get a job (1–3 response) or send him to five hours of maths grinds per week for the next two years (8–10 response), the chances are the right response is somewhere in the middle.

The core task of parenting is to make yourself redundant. When your children no longer need you, you have done your job

well. By coaching your child to behave in the 4–7 zone, reacting to adversity in a 4–7 manner, and allowing your children
to prioritise what is and is not important to them, you will be
teaching them to be resilient, self-assured and capable, and
that's what's going to stand to them the most as they enter the
choppy waters of adulthood.

Cognition

In terms of cognition, it is important to distinguish separate
aspects of the thinking process when it comes to children and
parents. One concerns the intellectual and developmental
aspects of cognition, which are an indication of a child's ability to understand, process and express information. The other
could be described as emotional cognition, which is more to do
with the manner in which the child thinks about themselves.

Intellectual and developmental cognition are important
when it comes to parenting roles. Despite well-known developmental milestones and developmental trajectories, parents still
seem unclear as to what cognitive level their child may be at
when it comes to certain points in their lifespan. For example,
I have had many parents describe expectations of their children
that are far beyond their developmental capacity and, as a result,
the interventions or the manner in which the parent is communicating with the child or young teenager is lost on them.
The most common example of this might be in small children
where parents seem exasperated that their child is not able to
follow instructions, and they interpret this non-compliance as

disobedience. When you hear the level of expectation that some parents place on small children, it becomes clear that the child just does not understand what is being asked of them, or that what is being asked is beyond their developmental capacity, and the parental expectation is in the 8–10 zone.

Similarly, parents can get frustrated at a teenager's lack of organisation, motivation to study or ability to plan into the future. Often parents in these situations describe teenagers as lazy, disinterested or resistant, when in reality they are simply unable to view their world through the lens of future planning because they are teenagers. The nature of adolescence is experimentation, and they are in the process of 'finding themselves'. This brings with it a degree of preoccupation, distraction and avoidance. This is not pathological; it is developmental. Many contemporary parents view adolescence as an 'apprenticeship for adulthood', but it is not.

Teenagers are not supposed to be able to be organised and make sensible decisions about their futures. They are 'in the moment' and often fearful of the future and the responsibilities that getting older entails. Parents often come to me explaining that their teenage boy won't study for his exams and instead sits on a gaming console chatting with his friends. Meanwhile, his parents are pulling their hair out and arguing with him all the time. The one thing you cannot do as a parent is make someone learn. They have to choose to do that themselves. You can lock a teenager in a room for hours with nothing but school textbooks, but even that does not guarantee that they will read them. In all my years of working with families in this situation, I have never seen a situation where persistent nagging and argument have led to positive behavioural change. They simply don't work. But because, as parents, we believe it is the only strategy we have, it is what we use. The only benefit of nagging and arguing is as a venting exercise for parents. It does nothing to motivate the teenager to comply with the parental demands. The most effective strategy is to try to incentivise the teenager to engage in more study. This seems counterproductive, but it will be more effective than nagging and arguing.

The most important aspect of childhood cognition is that parents are able to distinguish between a child who is 'unwilling' and a child who is 'unable'. This is crucial, because it will guide your approach to supporting your child. There is nothing worse than a child being chastised for something they are unable to do. Take a child who has poor eyesight, but this is undetected, and the child is genuinely struggling to see the words on the teacher's board to write them down on their page. The teacher notices that the child is not getting the task done in the time that others are and assumes they are lazy or resistant. The child is disciplined and sanctioned for being 'unwilling' to follow the teacher's instructions, when in reality they are unable. This process serves to damage the child's self-worth, as they believe they must be 'stupid' if they can't do it as fast as everyone else. It also serves to damage their relationship with school and education, which could lead to their being difficult and acting out, or giving up and zoning out.

There are other incidences where a child's cognitive capacity is underestimated. In these instances, a child will not learn to problem-solve or overcome challenges because they have not been given the opportunity. We have all heard of the 'helicopter' or 'snowplough' parenting approaches that are characterised by the parent being overinvolved in the child's life. If a child or teenager is not permitted to take on challenges that are appropriate to their developmental level, they will not have the opportunities to learn the skills to help them to navigate life. A teenager who has never been permitted to use public transport, be responsible for the key to the family home or purchase something from a shop will lose out on developing these life skills. Parents who are overinvolved in the teenager's decisions – for example, selecting the subjects they should choose for their senior cycle or filling out their college application forms – compromise the teenager in their becoming an adequate decision-maker as a young adult and thereby leave them vulnerable.

The parenting approach that expects too much of children from a cognitive perspective and leaves it all up to the child is a 1–3 approach, whereas the parent who is overinvolved and taking too much control of a child's decision-making process is engaged in an 8–10 approach. The 4–7 zone approach involves being aware of your child's cognitive capacity and ensuring that your interventions are appropriate. If you notice that your instructions are not having an impact on your child's behaviour, then it is important that you explore whether or not they understand and that you decipher whether they are unwilling or unable. This will guide all further interventions. If you feel that you are overinvolved in your child's decision-making and prohibiting them from becoming adequate decision-makers, then you need to step back and allow them to be cognitively challenged.

Emotions

One of the core aspects of childhood is emotional regulation, and this is a great challenge for many parents. As most parents will testify, there is nothing more heartbreaking than seeing your child upset. The emotional connection between parent and child can make it feel like you are experiencing emotional upset by proxy. The same applies when we observe our children experiencing joy – it can have a knock-on effect on our own positive emotions. So, the emotional rollercoaster of childhood can also result in an emotional rollercoaster for parents.

As previously highlighted, children and teenagers often have BIG emotions. The nature of their developmental stages is that they involve intense emotional experiences and reactions to even the seemingly most innocuous events. To observe a small child becoming inconsolably upset because their sibling chose the same flavour of crisps as them, or a teenager becoming distraught because their favourite pop band just broke up, may seem truly unbelievable. These reactions occur because the children are trying to come to terms with regulating their emotions. This is a process that takes time, needs ongoing support and only comes with maturity. There is no way of bypassing or skipping emotional regulation; it just has to be endured.

It is important not to underestimate the importance of emotional regulation. It is one of the core tasks of childhood and adolescence and plays a significant role in the child's developmental experience. Many of the difficulties that parents face in terms of childhood anxiety, low self-worth and tantrums occur because a child is struggling to regulate their emotions. It is also worth pointing out that although the struggle to emotionally regulate may not be obvious, that does not mean it's not happening. Returning to the concept of the internalising and externalising personality types, we might say that although the internaliser may not be overtly demonstrating this struggle, they may well be experiencing it internally through emotional rumination. Ideally, we want our children to be able to select what emotional experiences need to be externalised and internalised.

This is best taught through role modelling. Children learn how to regulate from their experiences of it, so as a parent you become a template for their emotional regulation. What we as parents choose to openly remonstrate over, and what we choose to keep to ourselves, will influence our children's subsequent behaviour. Encouraging a child to verbalise and externalise certain emotions and to tone down or internalise other emotional expressions is a long-term intervention, but if it is carried out in the spirit of the 4–7 zone, it will reap dividends for both parent and child. It is important to remember that no child is spared the task of emotional regulation, it just seems that it comes easier to some children compared with others, and therefore the amount of role modelling required will vary from child to child. There are ways in which parents can assist their children to regulate their emotions, and the 4–7 zone is an ideal template to assist with this process.

It is important to acknowledge that emotions are dynamic and reciprocal, which means they interact with each other, The emotional expression of the parent therefore impacts the emotional expression of the child and vice versa. There are some parenting approaches that recommend that parents need to be softly spoken and robot-like when interacting with an emotional child. I don't subscribe to that approach. The experience of being a parent is an emotional one, and when your child is having a massive tantrum and being really challenging, it is utterly unreasonable to expect a parent to be completely calm in that situation. When we set an expectation that you should never raise your voice or get cross with your child, all we do is increase the experience of parental guilt and make parents feel like they are failing. I would also question what the child learns from a parent who is completely emotionless in these scenarios. I believe children learn from feedback, and at times need to be made aware that their behaviour is upsetting those around them. However, it is necessary to try to not let this boil over into losing your cool or composure too much. The parent, as the adult in the room, needs to role model a 4–7 approach, or at least role model how the child can work towards moving back into the 4–7 zone even if this is not possible in the heat of the moment.

When a child is experiencing emotional upset, whether that is expressed through tantrums, tearfulness or silence, there are a series of possible responses. One response is to get consumed by their upset and become equally upset yourself. This could mean you get overinvolved in the scenario and react either by mirroring their anger or just sharing their level of upset. This is an 8–10 zone response. The second possible response is to try to dismiss the child's experience by telling them to 'get a grip' or that they are overreacting, or by trying to distract them away from what is upsetting them. This is a 1–3 zone response. While we may think that this is helpful because we are not buying into their anger or upset, what it tends to communicate is that you are not validating their emotions, and this can lead to an escalation or 'upping the ante' in order to be heard. The ideal response is to try to acknowledge how they are feeling but suggest other more adaptive ways that they can manage their upset. This would be the 4–7 zone response. While acknowledging how idealistic this might sound, if you find you are unable to achieve this level of measured response, perhaps it is a good idea to call in support from another parent or family member if this is possible.

To explain this process, I will describe 'the Well Metaphor' I use to illustrate to student mental health nurses how to manage highly charged emotional situations.

Imagine the upset individual is stuck in a large hole
and can't find their way out and you come upon the
scene. They are acutely distressed, crying and shout-
ing, and are a combination of upset and angry.

The first option is to approach the edge of the
hole, look down and say, 'Oh, you are stuck in a
hole. That's unfortunate, but there are people out
there in worse situations. Stop whining about it.'
This is a 1–3 zone approach and is ineffective. What
do you think the chances are of that person saying,
'You know, you're right. What have I got to be com-
plaining about? Thank you. I feel better now.' Highly
unlikely. What is far more likely to happen is that the
person who is stuck in the hole will just get angrier
and more upset.

The second option is to approach the edge of the
hole and look down and say, 'Oh my God, you are
stuck in a hole, you poor thing. Let me help', and so
you jump into the hole too. This is an 8–10 response.
All that has happened here is that now you are both
stuck in the hole, and although the person whom
you were trying to help may feel validated and experience your sympathy, you are completely ineffective
in helping them.

The third option is to say, 'Oh my God, you are
stuck in a hole! Hang on and I'll go get some help.'
When you return with the other person, you use

them to anchor you and lower you down some of the way. When you are able to communicate, you try to acknowledge the person's upset but explain how they will need to be a little calmer so you can help get them out. You cannot pull someone out of upset forcibly; instead, you must help them to help themselves. By offering helpful instructions – 'Put your foot on that ledge and reach up to my hand' – you are able to offer useful advice and stay grounded by the person acting as your anchor. This is the 4–7 zone approach.

An important distinction when it comes to assisting someone with emotional difficulties is that none of us can offer 'cures'; all we can do is 'offer support to facilitate change'. This is one of the hardest but most important realisations as a psychotherapist. Someone once explained to me that we are all 'responsible *to*' other people. We are responsible for being helpful, supportive and courteous and kind. But we can never be 'responsible *for*' other people. Despite our best efforts, every individual has the capacity to choose to listen and accept our advice or cover their ears and ignore it, and that is often beyond our control. One of the mistakes parents of older teens can make is that they don't accept that these young adults have the capacity to choose, and so our support should involve enticing and incentivising them to make good choices and not trying to control their decisions.

Overall, the most effective way that parents can support their children and teenagers to emotionally regulate is by role modelling good emotional self-management. This does not have to involve being robotic and softly spoken all the time; instead, it is about learning how to respond to your child's emotions instead of reacting to them. If on occasion you do react in the 8–10 or 1–3 zone, which is utterly understandable, it is important to try to address this and follow it up with a 4–7 response when you are ready.

The classic moment where we overreact in an emotional state is when we 'overcompensate' with punishment threats. This is when we are so annoyed that we make threats like 'you are grounded for a year', which is far too severe a consequence and also impossible to follow through on. This is a classic 8–10 reaction. However, when you have calmed down and emotionally regulated yourself, you may return to the young person and explain how upset or annoyed you were at their behaviour, but that maybe you didn't manage your reaction as well as you could have and so the revised sanction is that they are grounded for a weekend as opposed to the year that you previously threatened. It is good for children and teenagers to observe their parents own their own mistakes, especially the ones that occur in high-level emotional situations. It is a great example to the child or teenager that they too can make mistakes, but it is how you respond to those mistakes or emotional outbursts that is important. This consolidates the family value system of honesty, openness and authenticity.

CONCLUSION

Everything children and teenagers do tends to be in the 1–3 and 8–10 zones. This is just how they function. They are learning to regulate their emotions and behaviour by developing a capacity to think about and process these dynamics. As they are only in the process of developing, they will inevitably get this wrong from time to time. Their behaviour and their emotional reactions will be extreme. It is the role of the parent to absorb these experiences and offer learning opportunities for the child to manage them better. When we role model measured responses, we offer opportunities for the child to develop a language and understanding of emotion, which will mean they will rely less heavily on behaviour to communicate. By espousing the values that you want for your family, you create a culture that has a significant influence on your child's moral development.

One suggestion I have is that families are established more on strong values than rigid rules. As parents, we can become consumed with control, which can go either way with children. It can cause them to buck against it or to internalise it within themselves. Rather than our parental focus being on control, it may need to move towards guidance and steering. Allowing children to make mistakes and get things wrong, within reason, may be the most important learning experience of their lives. Let's not remove that from them for our own convenience.

CHAPTER TEN

Managing Anxiety

As previously stated, anxiety is the fear of the unknown. When we are anxious, there are three possible responses: fight, flight and freeze. Two of these are 'action' responses (fight or flight) and the other is an 'inaction' response (freeze). The action responses can be traditionally understood as getting angry or running away, and the inaction response involves becoming immobilised, but there are other responses that I believe can fall into these categories.

PERFECTIONISM

One action response that is becoming an increasingly common way to attempt to manage anxiety is 'perfectionism'. In the face of the overwhelming 'unknowns', perfectionism is an attempt to try to establish as many 'knowns' as possible. This can be observed in people who engage in over-preparation, frantic list-making or designing rigid timetables and timelines. People who have leanings towards these types of behaviours are commonly described as 'control freaks', or sometimes people can describe them as being quite 'anal' about things. This term derives from the Freudian interpretation of the 'anal stage of development', where Freud described some children as 'anally retentive' – typically children who hold onto their bowel movements during the potty-training phase because they cannot tolerate the 'mess' of defecation. This personality trait of not being able to tolerate any mess is often assigned to people who invest heavily in getting things to be perfect and who are intolerant of imperfection, which is the major flaw in this approach to anxiety. It is all very well and good when things are going perfectly to plan, but when adversity strikes and perfection is not possible, this approach can tend to fall apart.

The premise for perfectionism as a coping strategy is that perfectionism attempts to create as many knowns as possible in the face of the unknown. This approach to managing anxiety is helpful to a point. It helps, in the short term, to make someone feel less anxious, less unprepared and more ready for what possibly might happen. However, when it is overused, it will create more anxiety than it resolves. The more certainty we try to place on a period of uncertainty, the more likely we are to become overwhelmed when it does not go to plan. So, if there is an unanticipated disruption to the planned timetable, or if the list is becoming overwhelming, we tend to get more anxious, not because we are doing wrong, but because we are not able to follow the plan that we had devised.

Perfectionism is by its very nature unrealistic. In most aspects of life, a perfect outcome is not possible. Perfectionism is only effective when it comes to 'controllable variables', but in many situations this is only part of the challenge. The uncontrollable variable is often the more decisive one when it comes to determining an outcome. But we don't accept this realisation, as it contains a degree of uncertainty, and so we set a goal to achieve the perfect outcome.

Inevitably, the perfect plan will fail. However, rather than admitting that the approach didn't work and looking at an alternative strategy for the next challenge that life presents, perfectionistic people tend to believe that it didn't work because they 'just didn't do it perfectly enough'. And so they double down on their perfectionistic approach, thereby doubling the intensity of the goal-setting and application to the next task, and in turn doubling the inevitable disappointment that will occur – and so the cycle continues.

The popularity of perfectionism may be due in part to the evolution of technology. In a cut-and-paste world of filters and editing, there is a belief that perfectionism is not only possible but expected. Perhaps we believe that the capability to cultivate perfect imagery is transferable into our emotional lives. One thing I have learned as a psychotherapist, however, is that emotions are not neat. They are messy, unwieldy and unpredictable, and sometimes the more we try to control them the more unmanageable they become.

AVOIDANCE

The second way of coping with anxiety is an inaction response like avoidance. This is where we actively avoid facing anxiety-provoking events altogether. Again, this offers some short-term relief from anxiety, because we're not faced with having to challenge the stimulus that causes us anxiety. But in the longer term, this inaction response does not address the cause of our anxiety, and the problem continues. Like perfectionism, when we continue to use avoidance as a coping strategy it doubles the challenge of facing the anxiety-provoking stimulus. The longer we avoid it, the harder it is to return.

I believe that the global pandemic of 2020 is in part responsible for the greater incidence of avoidance in recent years. During the lockdown period, we were encouraged to avoid each other and stay in our bubbles. While this was horrendously difficult for many people and caused huge mental distress across the globe, others seemed to thrive in this set of circumstances. The lockdowns allowed for what was previously deemed impossible to become possible. We realised that we could now work effectively from home and that productivity was not negatively impacted. We could be educated from home too without too much academic disruption. All of the 'that could never happen' claims were dispelled, leaving companies and educational facilities in the difficult position of trying to convince people to come back to the workplace or place of education when the transmission threat of COVID-19 had diminished. The period of the pandemic allowed people who were anxious or those who do not enjoy social situations to get what they wanted, and there has been a noticeable 'glorification' of this on social media.

However, it is my belief that while many got what they wanted, it was not what they needed. Avoidance became possible and in some cases an option. The arguments against long commutes and wasted time in the office were commonplace, the bottom line of productivity became the defensive position, and the counterargument of the value of social and emotional exposure was hard to sell. However, what has been revealed since then is that those worries were not too far off the mark. Since the pandemic, we have seen a rise in loneliness and social disconnection, and the incidence of social avoidance seems a far bigger problem for many people now than it did prior to 2020.

Another form of avoidance is to try to avoid a peak of anxiety. If someone has a specific fear or phobia of something, their anxiety will rise when there is a potential encounter with the feared stimulus. When trying to help someone with, for example, a phobia of dogs, their anxiety level might be 8/10 when a dog is around 15m away, it will rise to 9/10 when the dog is a metre away, and will peak at 10/10 when they reach out to touch the dog. However, as they remain in the position of touching the dog, yet the feared response – that is, that the dog will bite – does not happen, their anxiety begins to reduce over time to perhaps 9/10, then 8/10 and so on. So, what we know from this is that when we allow anxiety to peak and the feared response does not materialise, the anxiety will come down.

This principle is applicable to other feared situations, like socialising. Often if we are anxious about something and engaged in trying to avoid it, we can exist in a continuous state of moderately high anxiety, such as 8/10 or 9/10. While avoidance helps us never to reach the peak level of 10/10 anxiety, it never allows us to come down to the other side. This is critical: anxiety must peak to come down the other side. Therefore, avoidance never allows anxiety to peak and prohibits us from ever recovering. This is why it is appealing as a short-term strategy but is ineffective in the longer term.

With reference to the 4–7 zone, avoidance would be considered a 1–3 response, whereas perfectionism would be an 8–10 response. The reality is that the 4–7 response, which is ideal in this situation, involves not aiming to seek absolute certainty through perfectionism and not trying to bypass all anxiety through the response of avoidance. The 4–7 zone response involves gradually building up a tolerance of uncertainty and gradually exposing yourself to anxiety-provoking situations in a way that you can manage.

UNDERSTANDING ANXIETY
Biology

Let's first look at the biological influences of anxiety. Anxiety affects our sleep, appetite and motivation. Anxiety is one of the most visible components of mental distress in the body. When we are anxious, our body tenses up in response to threat or stress. For example, people with anxiety issues often experience physical symptoms such as irritable bowel syndrome, migraine, neck, shoulder or back pain, and rashes or skin reactions.

In acute levels of anxiety, in the panic phase, our heart rate goes up, we experience palpitations and we can start to sweat, especially on our palms. Our pupils can become dilated, and we can feel our bodies start to shake. This is because anxiety is very closely linked to our biology, so the first port of call in managing our anxiety is to try to influence the reaction in our bodies.

Some people who experience acute levels of anxiety may take medications to help to manage panic attacks. These medicines are known as benzodiazepines, and while they are effective in reducing the physiological experience of a panic attack, they are also very addictive. Benzodiazepine use should only be a feature of anxiety treatment when the panic experience is very acute and when the other non-pharmacological interventions have not worked.

There are many non-pharmacological or natural ways in which we can effectively manage our body's response to anxiety, such as breathing techniques, relaxation exercises and meditation or mindfulness. For people who are more 'active relaxers', the option of sea swimming or playing five-a-side football can also serve the same purpose. There are many ways in which we can find our 'zone' when it comes to switching on or switching off, and we should all explore ways that suit our own leanings as opposed to trying to force ourselves to fit a popular approach.

Psychology

Our psychological mindset plays a large role in our experience of anxiety. There are people who could be described as having an anxious temperament, and those people tend to see everything through the lens of threat rather than opportunity.

An example of someone like that might be a friend of mine, Mary. I have known Mary almost all of my life, and Mary has always had an anxious temperament. An example of how Mary sees the world was noticeable last year when Mary and I visited another friend who had moved into a beautiful new home. Our friend was keen to show Mary and me her new home, which was a beautiful old Georgian house that had huge ceilings and fabulous open living spaces.

When our friend had finished the tour of her new home, which she was clearly excited about, Mary didn't say, 'Oh, this is a beautiful home,' like I expected. Instead she said, 'Are you not worried about how you are going to afford to heat this place?'

For me, this response by Mary was a perfect example of someone who is seeing the world through the lens of threat. While it seems from her reaction that she is being quite negative, she is not. Mary is a wonderful person who loves to witness joy in others, but she is also someone who has a tendency for anxious thinking patterns, and this is just one example of how these can manifest.

The tendency to see experiences through the lens of threat or opportunity can be a temperament issue, but it can also be created through a series of negative experiences. If you have witnessed or experienced disappointment, betrayal or trauma, this can create a lens of anxiety through which all future experiences might be viewed. If you have been involved in a car accident, you may become a nervous passenger. If you have experienced disappointment, you may tend to fear hope, and if you have been betrayed, you might feel anxious about trusting people. All of these reactions are understandable within these contexts, but that does not mean that they cannot be challenged, changed or improved.

Social

Anxiety is commonly associated with social situations or perceived social pressures. The social environment is by its nature quite unpredictable, and therefore contains a lot of unknowns. To counter these unknowns, anxious people can choose to avoid social situations or try to control them. We can avoid social situations by simply not engaging or accepting any social invitations. We may try to control social situations by requesting to work from home rather than go into the office. Alternatively, we may feel we need some alcohol in order to manage or survive a social evening.

Behaviour

Anxiety can have a significant influence on our behaviours. As well as keeping us awake at night ruminating over banal and innocuous events that might happen, it can also turn us off our food or cause us to comfort-eat to keep uncomfortable feelings at bay. Anxiety can make us awkward in social situations or overwhelmed at the prospect of having to give a presentation at work, or even cause us to make three separate trips back to our bedroom to make sure we have plugged out the hair straightener before we leave the house.

However, the behaviours we engage in to attempt to manage anxiety can also be problematic. I am always interested to hear about children who go to great lengths to convince their parents they are ill in order to not go to school. The effort and planning that go into avoiding going to school seem to far exceed the effort required to go in. This speaks to the significance of the anxiety they are experiencing, and the extent of the avoidance strategies seems to mirror the intensity of the anxious feelings. Most behaviours are employed as coping strategies. Whether it is making a list or drinking a bottle of whiskey, both are trying to achieve the same outcome: to reduce anxiety. As discussed previously, the behavioural response to anxiety is either an active response – to try to control the unknown variables – or an inactive one, which serves to avoid the anxiety-provoking situation.

Cognition

The non-pharmacological interventions mentioned earlier are also useful for managing cognitive reactions to anxiety. The experience of physiological symptoms of anxiety like sweaty palms and palpitations can trigger cognitive catastrophising.

This is where our thoughts can run away from us and start to sow seeds in our minds that this is going to end in disaster. Cognitive catastrophic thoughts can include things like 'you are having a heart attack', 'everyone is looking at you' or 'you are going red and everyone is laughing at you'. These thoughts only serve to trigger further physiological anxiety, so your heart will beat faster, your palms will become sweatier, and your face will go even redder. This is adding cognitive fuel to the fire of anxiety and risks a blaze of panic. The key management strategy is to try to regain control over your thoughts and stem the flow of the lighter fluid (thoughts) onto the flames (biological symptoms).

The other cognitive pattern that is problematic is the rumination loop. This is where our cognitive activity goes into overdrive, and we attempt to forensically analyse every situation in our lives. When we feel anxiety in our bodies, we believe this is a 'sign' that something bad is going to happen. We listen to our 'gut' and attempt to find out what the potential threat could be. This involves overthinking all aspects of our lives to try to identify the source of our anxiety. The faulty thinking position here is that we believe that because we *feel* something is going to happen, well then it *is* going to happen. However, when we are anxious, our feelings are utterly unreliable and they create feelings and fears that do not – and need not – exist. The realisation that 'a feeling is not a fact' escapes us, and we ruminate over every minute detail of our lives to try to identify the source of threat, which creates more anxious feelings of impending doom, thereby agitating our anxious hunch and increasing the need to ruminate even more. Developing an ability to interrupt the cognitive rumination loop is an essential component of trying to manage our experiences of anxiety.

Emotions

While the biological effect of anxiety is distressing and problematic, and the cognitive response is crucial to whether the experience gets better or worse, we tend to overlook the emotional impact of anxiety. As discussed earlier, emotions are hard to control and influence, and we tend to try to make changes in thoughts and behaviours instead, as they are somewhat more tangible and open to change. However, the role of emotion is important, because it tends to be the fuse that is lit which later leads to the explosion of cognitive and biological anxious reactions.

One thing we can do is try to be aware of the process of 'emotional reasoning'. Emotional reasoning occurs when we mistake a feeling for a fact, and why we do this is understandable. We are told all our lives about the importance of intuition and hunches and listening to our gut. There is some degree of belief that our bodies have an almost sixth sense when it comes to danger. A bit like the tales of animals heading for the high ground before a weather disaster, it is sometimes believed that humans have this ability to identify potential danger. However, when we are in a state of anxiety, our antenna for danger malfunctions. It sees potential danger in everything. It will try to convince our mind that all aspects of our environment hold catastrophic risks and will try to get us to behave in a way to defend against all of these possibilities.

While these misfiring emotions are very real, and how we react and respond to them is crucial, there is another aspect to the role of emotion that is not discussed adequately, and this is the long-term emotional impact of being an anxious person. Over time, anxiety can be exhausting. It leaves us feeling useless, defeated and unable to manage the world. It is this emotional response that comes at a great cost to people who suffer from anxiety because of the impact it has on their self-worth and self-value. Anxiety can deplete these aspects over time, leaving the person feeling unable to manage life and the world. This can result in apathy, avoidance and low mood.

Anxiety is like having an internal critic on your shoulder, talking in your ear all the time, telling you that you are 'not able', that 'you will fail' or that others 'don't like you'. Being constantly exposed to this negative and critical voice can have a significant and enduring impact on our emotions and on our will and desire to do something about it.

AVA

Ava was a 28-year-old woman who presented for treatment of anxiety. She described struggling with 'worry' since her teenage years, but said she was always able to 'get by'. In recent months

it had got worse, however. She had an interview for a promotion coming up that she really wanted, but she felt her anxiety
would prevent her from getting the job, so she decided to try
to seek some support.

Biology

Upon assessment, it was clear that Ava was doing well biologically. Her diet was good and she engaged in regular exercise.
However, her sleep was a problem, and she reported spending
hours trying to turn off her thoughts at night to try to get to
sleep. This left her tired the next day and less able to challenge
her anxious thoughts. While her diet and exercise levels were
5/10, her sleep pattern was 2/10.

Psychology

Despite struggling with worry since she was a teenager, Ava had
no other obvious trauma in her life. She had a supportive family
and lots of friends, she was bright, and she enjoyed her job.
However, she did say that her mother was always very anxious
and remains so to this day. Ava's mother sounded like she had
struggled with anxiety all her life, but this was never diagnosed.
Ava's mother rings her around five times a day to enquire how
she is doing and to offload her own anxieties on Ava. Ava finds
this exhausting, but cannot ask her mother to stop doing it for
fear it will make her mother more anxious.

This relationship dynamic between Ava and her mother
seemed to be a far bigger issue than Ava recognised and was

clearly making her more anxious. Ava said that even when her mother wasn't on the phone, Ava was constantly waiting for her to call and couldn't 'switch off' from it. This relationship was maintaining Ava's vigilance and anxiety, and was 8/10 in terms of intensity. Ava's self-worth was really low. She lacked self-belief and was unable to list four 'good qualities' about herself. I felt her self-value was 2/10.

Social

Ava visited her mother every day on the way home from work and would call over on the weekends. Ava had some friends from work, but they lived on the other side of the city, so they did not meet up regularly. Ava was not in a relationship and reported not having 'any interest in dating'. Further exploration revealed that Ava would quite like a romantic relationship, but she was anxious that no one would find her attractive. She did not want to 'put herself out there' for fear of rejection, so she made excuses that she was too busy with her 'job' and 'minding her mother'. Despite Ava's friendship network seeming to be in the 4–7 zone in terms of the number of friends, the quality of her actual physical relational experiences was 2/10.

Behaviour

Ava's 'go-to' response to anxiety was avoidance. She had skilfully convinced herself that this was just because she was 'too busy', but this was an excuse and not an explanation. Ava made herself busy so that she would not have time for things she found daunting. This may have been unconscious, but it seems that for most of her life Ava had been avoiding things and explaining that this was for practical reasons. Ava's engagement in life was 3/10 and her avoidance tendency was 9/10.

Cognition

Ava's thought patterns were clearly problematic. She explained that she would ruminate over almost everything. Small, insignificant conversations with colleagues during the day would be unpicked in great detail at night to examine what she had said that could be interpreted as foolish. Ava was dominated by a lens of threat and saw most social opportunities as a chance of her 'making a mess of things'. Her anxious cognition lens was 8/10.

Emotions

Ava was not aware of how sad she actually was in her life. The busy job and rushing over to her mother's at every spare minute distracted her from her own loneliness. It was easier for Ava to lie awake at night forensically examining a water-cooler conversation with a colleague that day than to contemplate her own feelings of isolation and her fear of being alone forever. Ava's emotional well-being was 2/10.

Now let's use the 4–7 zone to illustrate how it can be used to help with feelings of anxiety.

MAKING CHANGES

Upon hearing Ava's story, it was my opinion that her cognitive issues were causing her to stay awake at night and were negatively impacting her biological well-being, and that they were also playing a role in her avoidance of social relationships. Therefore, that is where I believed the work of addressing Ava's anxiety needed to start, with cognitive rewiring.

Cognitive Rewiring

Ava's cognitive pathways were very established, as she had thought this way since she was a teenager. I was unsure whether this was a learned behaviour from her mother or a temperament issue. Regardless of the origin, her negative thinking patterns needed to be challenged. I am not a fan of setting people homework in therapy, but I do ask them to 'tune in to' certain aspects of their lives and try to increase their awareness of their habits.

I explained to Ava that anxious people do two things. They overestimate the challenge and they underestimate their own ability. This is because the anxious voice in their head tries to get them to see things this way. For example, Ava's thoughts about the upcoming interview in work were that if she did not get this job, people would think she was useless and she would have to leave, and if she was lucky enough to get the job, she would not be able for it. This is an example of anxiety convincing Ava that she should overestimate the challenge and underestimate her ability. Therefore, Ava saw the challenge as 9/10 and her ability to manage it as 1/10. This was the first cognitive pathway to address.

We considered the challenge of the job interview, but I insisted that Ava only discuss this using facts, not feelings. I explained that facts are things that would stand up in a court of law, but feelings do not. If a judge asked a witness why they stated that 'Man A killed Man B', the witness could not say, 'Well, because I feel like he did.' Feelings are not facts, and so the discussion could only be had using facts.

Ava was unable to defend why she would not get the job when we removed the influence of feelings. As it turned out, basing the discussion on facts alone made a convincing argument for why Ava should get the job. She was more than qualified for the role. She had more experience than other candidates and she had a strong reputation in the company, based on her feedback reviews, not her opinion. Ava was also unable to underestimate her own ability when we reduced the conversation to facts alone. She actually inadvertently reminded herself of her own value as the discussion unfolded. This process of 'demanding the evidence' is an effective way to challenge anxious thoughts and remind someone of their own ability. We surmised that Ava's interpretation of the challenge of the job interview was 9/10 and that this needed to be brought back into the 4–7 zone. Her belief in her own ability was 1/10, and this needed to be raised into the 4–7 zone.

The next aspect that we needed to address was Ava's social world. We explored the impact of the relationship she had with her mother, and while it seemed that Ava's mother was overly dependent on Ava and she was very supportive of her mother, her mother still often subjected her to a lot of criticism. Her mother would constantly ask her why she was not in a relationship and often passed comments on Ava's appearance. It turned out that the interactions Ava had with her mother mostly left her feeling deflated and upset. Her mother also confirmed a lot of Ava's anxieties by suggesting that Ava 'wouldn't be able for that' when it came to things like the promotion Ava was applying for.

We agreed that Ava's involvement in her mother's life and vice versa was too much and rated it as 9/10. This needed to reduce to the 4–7 zone. Ava was supported to make the brave step and tell her mother that she needed more space. Despite this being a real challenge for Ava, she did articulately assert her own needs. While her mother was not initially impressed, she soon came around to the idea, and the fallout was far less than what Ava had imagined in her own mind. Ava's corresponding guilt about stepping back from her relationship with her mother was 9/10, and this needed to be reduced too. Ava's social involvement with her peers was 2/10, and we needed to increase this to the 4–7 zone. From an emotional, psychological and biological perspective, I believed that if Ava could address the cognitive aspects of her anxiety and manage her social relationships better, at the same time reducing her exposure to her mother's negativity, it would have a positive impact on all of the other areas.

Over the next month, Ava made a concerted effort to engage only in fact-based thoughts, and to reduce her opinions or feelings in her internal conversations in her head. While she recognised that this was really difficult, with time and perseverance she made some progress. Ava tried really hard not to overestimate the challenges in her life and to nourish her belief in her own ability. This was a game-changer, and returning these thinking patterns into the 4–7 zone really helped. Ava liked the fact that the 4–7 zone was not trying to make her do a complete flip on who she was. Ava's self-worth was so low that trying to convince her to 'love herself', which some of the self-help books had proposed, was a leap too far. All I was looking for Ava to do was to cut herself some slack. I was not looking for her to stand in front of the mirror every morning and tell herself she was amazing.

The 4–7 zone worked for Ava because it was practical. She had downloaded every meditation and mindfulness app known to humanity over recent years, but she wanted some direction as to what she needed to do, and more importantly, how much was enough. This is the beauty of the 4–7 zone. It is just about tweaking what we think and do so that we can give our emotions a chance to change. It does not call for any epiphanies or life-changing action; it is simply a case of doing less of one thing and doing more of something else.

As Ava ruminated less, her social world increased at the same time. Pushing herself to meet up with friends was challenging to begin with, but after a while it was very beneficial. This, combined with less time being exposed to her mother's anxiety, was hugely helpful in offering her belief that things could be different. Change does not occur in the therapy room. It occurs when you take the insights outside into the world and make changes. These corrective emotional experiences are the catalysts for change, not insightful conversations with someone like me.

As it turned out, Ava did not apply for the job. Instead, she decided to take a year out and travelled to a friend who was based in Canada. This was a huge leap for Ava, but when she had made the initial move to step back from her intense relationship with her mother, she realised that her mother was far more capable and industrious than she had thought. It was almost like Ava's involvement with her mother was creating a learned helplessness, and when she stepped back, her mother proved to be far more capable than even she herself had imagined. The success of stepping back from that relationship, which Ava had never deemed possible, gave her the confidence to pursue her own desires. While this move was very anxiety provoking, Ava was on a roll in terms of her decision-making, and she bravely took a huge risk and went for it. Her friend organised another similar job for Ava, and so she went. When I last heard from her, she was still in Canada and doing well. She said she still drifts into the 1–3 and 8–10 zones from time to time but tries not to stay there too long, and that's good enough for me.

PART THREE

Becoming Your Own Therapist

CHAPTER ELEVEN

The Meaning of Behaviour

So, now you know all about the 4–7 zone. You've learned about how it is easy to fall into habits of overdoing and underdoing certain aspects of our lives like our work–life balance; our sleep, diet and exercise; and our relationship with technology. Hopefully, you have also been able to identify areas of your life where you might benefit from making some changes. However, there's a difference between *knowing* what to do and *actually doing it*. You may be aware that an aspect of your life is in the 1–3 or 8–10 zone, but actually doing something about it is another matter.

This chapter will aim to add another layer to your awareness of your own behaviour by exploring the influence of our feelings on our behaviours. We may be able to take a step back and know what it is we are doing that could potentially be causing us added stress, but it is also helpful to understand 'why' we might be engaging in these behaviours, and sometimes that insight is not obvious. Often the motivating factor for 'why' we do certain things or why certain things provoke disproportionately strong reactions for us is our 'feelings'. Our feelings often determine how we react to events in our lives and have a far more influential impact on our actions than most of us realise. Even if we do realise that we need to make a change, putting this knowledge into action or creating behavioural change can be a lot more difficult. This chapter will explore possibilities for why we might behave the way we do, and better equip us to engage in meaningful behavioural change.

THE BATTLE BETWEEN THE THINKING MIND AND THE FEELING MIND

We do not base our decisions solely on what we think or know, but on what we feel. While we would like to believe that we are all quite rational, measured and thinking individuals, we are not. Nobody functions solely from a thinking perspective: feelings always play a significant role in all of our decision-making, and it is important to recognise and acknowledge the influence of this dynamic. For the purposes of explanation, I will refer to the 'thinking mind' and the 'feeling mind'. It is also important to realise that many of the reasons why we might struggle to manage aspects of our lives involve the emotional reactions that life events provoke in us, and that in many cases successfully navigating these life stresses involves managing our reaction or response to the incident, in addition to managing the practicalities of what has happened. Therefore, integrating the 4–7 zone into our emotional reactions to events will prove hugely helpful as we attempt to manage life's challenges.

These concepts are commonly misunderstood because it is convenient for us to misunderstand them. We talk about the importance of 'awareness' and 'education' as a means of responding to all of life's struggles and see this as the panacea to all our personal and societal problems. This assumes that 'knowing' is key to change, and this would be true if we only had a thinking mind that based all decisions on knowledge. However, in addition to our thinking mind, we also have a feeling mind, and this complicates matters. The thinking mind is the rational, measured and reasonable part of our personality. It is informed, logical and calm. It is the part of our mind that weighs up pros and cons and bases decisions on facts and prob-ability. By contrast, the emotional mind is impulsive, reactive and instinctive. It is volatile, intense and imaginative. It is the part of our mind that seeks joy, pleasure and satisfaction and relies on hunches, gut feelings and intuition.

The interaction between our thinking mind and our emo-tional mind is most evident in our decision-making processes. The thinking and emotional minds are always competing with each other, vying to have the last word on the decisions we make in our lives. Most people believe that we are governed by our thinking mind and that our emotional mind is there in the background, trying – mostly unsuccessfully – to sway us to do something rash or reactive. When we wake up tired and don't want to go to work, our emotional mind suggests, 'Maybe I will just call in sick and stay in bed,' but then our thinking mind suggests, 'No. You need to do the right thing, so get out of bed and go to work.' However, it is my belief that the emotional mind is actually the dominant part of that relationship and therefore it is influencing the bulk of our decisions, while the thinking mind is in the background trying to sway our decisions to be more measured and responsive. It is like when a small child is taking a large dog for a walk on a lead. The child (the thinking mind) believes they are in control, whereas in reality, the large dog (the emotional mind) is dictating the route.

Let me explain.

Knowing something is right or wrong has little or no impact on our actual behaviour. *Knowing* something does not equate with *doing* something. For example, we all know that smoking and drinking alcohol are bad for our health, but many of us do them anyway. We know that we shouldn't watch that extra episode of the series we are watching on Netflix because it would be better for us to go to sleep and get some rest, but we do it anyway. We know, logically, that we should eat more greens and less junk food, but we don't, because knowing something does not dictate our decisions; feelings do. This is why advertising campaigns are most effective when they connect with our emotions. If we consider advertising campaigns that are aimed at increasing our awareness of road safety or drunk driving, we can observe that they focus on gory imagery to make us feel something about the behaviour, which aims to motivate us to act differently. The reverse advertisements at Christmastime are aimed at connecting with positive emotions like nostalgia or reminiscence that make the content relatable and strong.

THE MOTION OF EMOTION

Feelings and emotions are far more likely to instigate or paralyse action than thoughts do. The word 'emotion' even contains the term 'motion' in it, which suggests that it has some relationship with movement or change. We are more likely to be spurred into action in our lives because of our emotions, not because of our thoughts. If we meet anyone who has made some major lifestyle-changing decisions in their lives, they will often refer to 'a moment' where they were spurred into action and which involved an emotion as opposed to a thought. People don't usually tell you they were motivated to adopt a healthy diet and exercise because they read a leaflet in the waiting room of a GP surgery. It is more likely to be because they saw a photo of themselves, and how they perceived they looked in the photo triggered an emotional response which led to their lifestyle changes. People don't tend to give up harmful behaviours because someone suggested they should; they do it because they were provided with an emotional moment of clarity that sparked off a response.

Our emotions are important aspects of our behaviours and are in a lot more control of our actions than we would like to believe or admit. We do most things or we don't do most things not because we *know*, but because we *feel*. Procrastination is not a behavioural problem; it is an emotional problem.

Impulsiveness is not a behavioural problem; it is an emotional problem. Avoidance is not a behavioural or cognitive or social problem; it is an emotional one. We are often far more likely to base our actions on what feels right as opposed to what we think is right. With this in mind, you might think I am suggesting that self-control is an illusion, but I am not. While I think self-control is a valid concept and I believe it does play a role in determining our choices and actions, it is a lot less influential than we believe it to be. Many of us don't realise the power of the emotional mind in determining our actions and believe that we make decisions according to what we think we should do rather than what we feel we should do.

THE SUBTLETIES OF BEHAVIOUR

I have worked with many people over the years who have psychological issues that manifest into behavioural symptoms. These can include restrictive diets, overeating, self-harm, compulsive behaviours and addictions. When people who are experiencing these difficulties come to me for support, they already know that what they are doing is 'not the right thing' for them to be doing. They know that what they are doing is causing harm in the longer term. They know their behaviours are negatively affecting those around them. But simply 'knowing' all of this does not result in behavioural change. This is because knowledge plays a very small part in determining our actions and decisions. Feelings are also very important and play a key role in why they happen.

When people have conditions like anorexia nervosa, their family members and friends will often think, 'Why don't they just eat?', which shows that they have a limited understanding of the fact that the condition is not a behavioural problem but an emotional one. Similarly, in the case of someone who engages in obsessive rituals like handwashing, family members can get exasperated and say, 'He knows it's harming him. Why doesn't he just stop?', again showing the limit of their understanding that behaviours like these are not logical or rational and therefore the thinking mind is futile in the face of the overpowering emotional mind.

This dynamic can be applied to more everyday experiences too. For example, a spouse and children may plead with someone who smokes to give up smoking, and despite being acutely aware of every risk factor to their health, they continue to smoke. Despite the knowledge of its potential for harm and the heartfelt pleas from loved ones, the person cannot make that change. Another example is someone who is working very long hours and missing out on family and social experiences. Despite the knowledge that they will regret these missed opportunities in the future, they continue the same patterns. The reasons for their inability to change may lie far more in the realm of emotionality than in the realm of knowledge.

It is difficult to explain how our emotional minds can make a logical change so difficult. When explaining to family members who are struggling to see why someone is resistant to change when clearly their behaviour is damaging them so much,

I like to use what I call 'the Lifebuoy Metaphor' to explain the emotional dynamics at play when it comes to changing behaviour.

Imagine your emotional distress is akin to being lost at sea and the challenges life is presenting to you are like the waves around you, which are overwhelming you and throwing you around in the water. Imagine you come across a lifebuoy ring, and when you hold onto it, it helps you to stabilise. The lifebuoy ring could be any of these sets of behaviours: restriction of diet, overeating, alcohol, rituals or self-harm. Engaging in these behaviours seems to help you to regain some control over your emotions. They offer distraction and in an odd way some control. You now have something you can use to fend off the overwhelming power of the waves.

At a later time, concerned family members or mental health professionals arrive and offer some help. For the purpose of the metaphor, let us imagine they are in a small rowing boat and are offering to bring you to shore, to a place of safety. At first you are relieved, but as you are boarding the small rowing boat, they tell you that you must discard the lifebuoy ring in order to get in the boat. This causes you concern. Why would you discard the one and only thing that helped you? There is an emotional attachment to the lifebuoy ring now, and you realise, when you must let it go, just how important it is to you. So instead of discarding the lifebuoy ring, you choose to decline the offer to board the small rowing boat and instead return to the water.

Over the next number of months or years, the small rowing boat returns many times offering to bring you ashore under the same conditions, but your anxiety about giving up the lifebuoy ring means that you continue to decline and stay floating in the water. As time passes, the shore begins to look less like a place of sanctuary and more like a location to be feared. Because you have been away from the shore for so long, it is now a place that is associated with fear, responsibility, expectation and anxiety.

People in this situation are not resistant to change; they fear it. It is very difficult to realise, when you are in the water, that the thing you believe is saving you (lifebuoy ring/problematic behaviour) is the thing that is actually drowning you. Also, the more you refuse to board the boat, the less likely the boat is to return, and some people will give up offering help, as they will see your fear as a reluctance to change and you as 'a lost cause'.

What might work better in this instance is if we allowed the person in the water, who is fearful of change, to take the lifebuoy ring with them onto the boat and then onto the shore. This removes the 'conditions of recovery'. If we allowed them to take it with them, then when they feel safe enough on the shore they might be better able to relinquish the lifebuoy ring of their own accord when they realise that they don't need it anymore, rather than being forced to surrender it when they have not been given anything to compensate for the loss of it. This approach does not demand that the person immediately stops their coping behaviour – overeating or alcohol dependency, for example – but instead seeks help to acquire alternative coping strategies so that bit by bit their behaviour will modify to a place where it eventually becomes redundant.

In this example, I recommend addressing the emotional mind issue in the first instance before expecting a behavioural change to occur. Too many treatment approaches are based on the belief that behavioural change must be the priority and must come first, but this does not consider the influence of the emotional mind over the thinking mind. Of course, sometimes we need to do something different to feel better, but we may also need support and more moderate expectations when we are trying to change. Small, gradual shifts in thinking and behaviour are far more likely to achieve sustainable change than extreme, dramatic 360-degree actions. We must also acknowledge that we engage in some things as a result of emotional and thinking dynamics, and sometimes it is best to try to unpick and understand these dynamics as we embark on trying to change them.

THE 'MEANING' BEHIND BEHAVIOUR

When we are trying to change a behaviour, it is important to first establish the 'meaning' behind the behaviour. It is my belief that every behaviour has meaning, no matter how obscure. If we cannot establish the meaning behind the behaviour, then we must try to at least create an honest evaluation of the 'function' of the behaviour, because every behaviour also always has a function.

A useful way of finding out the meaning of your behaviour is to ask yourself if the behaviour is a signpost to the problem as opposed to being the actual problem. For example, if you are struggling to sleep at night and this is leaving you tired and irritable during the day, you will say to yourself that your inability to sleep is the problem that requires fixing. You may then go to the pharmacy or health food store and buy lots of calming incense, herbal lavender drops and other sleep aids to resolve the problem. However, despite these interventions, your sleep is not improving.

Rather than seeing the problem as 'sleep', consider that your sleep is a signpost to other possible stressors. When you do this, you may realise that the timeline of your sleep problems coincides with a change in your life. Maybe it was a new role you took on in work; maybe it was since your child changed crèche; or maybe it was since you and your partner had that big argument. Whatever the reason, chances are that those circumstances are the reason for your poor sleep, and all the herbal drops in the world are not going to resolve that issue, because it is an emotional one. Maybe exploring the impact of the new role you have taken on in work, talking to someone about your underlying worries about your new childcare arrangements, or revisiting the discussion with your partner is more likely to improve your sleep, because your recent insomnia may not be the problem; instead, it is the signpost to the problem. Therefore, try not to take behaviours at face value. There are often other less obvious dynamics going on, and the current behavioural struggle is an indirect attempt to bring your attention to that issue.

Consider someone who has a problem with alcohol. Sometimes people tend to be interested in 'how much they drink', and while this may help to establish the extent of the problem, it does little to establish the depth of the problematic behaviour. Instead, we should be interested in 'why you drink'. The 'why' is looking at the meaning and function of the behaviour, and establishing this will speak to the depth of the problem. Someone may drink 20 units of alcohol a week, and this is a description of the extent of the problematic behaviour, but it does not illuminate anything about the origin of the problem. If we enquire about why someone started drinking, we might learn that they were feeling 'lonely', 'lost' or 'overwhelmed'. They may believe that alcohol seemed to help them to feel less like this in the short term. The origin of the problem is therefore loneliness and feeling overwhelmed, and the function of the behaviour is to alleviate or escape this feeling for a short period.

In many ways problematic behaviours do not always start out as *problems*; they often appear to start out as *solutions*. The best way to explain how a solution behaviour becomes a problem behaviour is to use the metaphor of 'the Miracle Cream'.

Let's imagine that emotional distress is a rash on your finger. When you engage in certain behaviours, like being preoccupied with food, weight and shape, or drinking alcohol, it acts like a miracle cream that makes the rash disappear almost instantly. You experience this as positive, as it allows you to escape your own ruminating thoughts and permits you to go about your day. But the next morning when you wake up, your whole hand is covered in the same rash as the day before, only worse – that is, the emotional distress returns, but it is now more intense. So, naturally you apply more of the miracle cream (or engage in the behaviour) that helped the previous day, and once again the rash is gone within a few minutes and the distress is less. But the following morning your whole arm is covered in the rash, and therefore even more cream is required and you engage even more intensely in the same behaviour. This continues until your whole body is covered in the rash and you become completely dependent on the cream and unable to function without it. The solution behaviour has now become a problem behaviour and

dependency has been created. You may not have the
rash anymore, but instead you are now completely
dependent on the miracle cream. You cannot leave
the house without the cream, and it is affecting your
relationships and everyday functioning.

The solution in this instance is to try to source the origin
of what is causing the rash (emotional pain) and then try to
reduce or wean off the cream (problem behaviour). The important information to establish in this instance is 'why' you need
to use the cream rather than 'how much cream you use'. Again,
this involves questioning what is, metaphorically, causing the
rash, rather than exploring ways to eliminate it. This involves
questioning whether the behaviour is the problem or merely a
signpost to the problem.

Family members are often guilty of seeing the behaviour as
the problem too, and this can be a further barrier to the realisation that it is not the problem but the signpost to the problem.
Family members can be very good at identifying the problem
for us, but not always able to see where the most meaningful
solution might need to happen. Most problematic behaviour we
experience first comes to the attention of our family and friends
because they recognise it is excessive (in the 8–10 zone), and it
may be clearly impacting our ability to function in the other
aspects of our lives, that is, socially or occupationally (in the
1–3 zone). Concerned observers and loved ones understandably
believe that our behaviour is problematic, and they offer advice

on how we should resolve it. For example, if a family member expresses concern about your drinking habits (8/10) and how they are impeding your ability to function in your everyday life (2/10), then the solution would seem to be to stop or reduce your drinking. However, we may not know *why* we are drinking alcohol in this way, so the demands of others to simply 'stop drinking' can make us feel misunderstood and even more alone, which may result in us engaging in even more excessive drinking behaviours that further impact on our daily functioning.

I have seen countless examples in my clinical career of people who gather around the symptom and see it as the totality of the problem, instead of paying attention to where it is pointing. If your fuel gauge light on your car comes on, it is an indication that you are running low on fuel and you need to get some more. The problem is not an issue with the light on the dashboard; it is the diminishing amount of fuel in the tank. However, to focus purely on the symptom and not see it as a signpost is to ask how we can get this fuel light to go out as opposed to what we can do to address the origin of the problem – that is, the lack of fuel.

Most, if not all, problematic behaviours that cause concern to others around us are noticeable because they are excessive. The person of concern is doing too much of something or too little of something. They are not functioning in the 4–7 zone. However, they are doing this for a reason, and it is important to try to understand that reasoning before jumping in with proposed solutions.

THE 3 C'S OF UNDERSTANDING BEHAVIOUR

Problematic behaviours like trying to over-control our food intake or binge eating, and even substance misuse or self-harm, all have a function. That function may not be very obvious to others around the person, but it is often the case. I will try to explain this process through the '3 C's of understanding behaviour'. The 3 C's of understanding behaviour are 'Cope', 'Control' and 'Communicate'. These are the most common reasons why people engage in excessive problematic behaviour.

Cope

We engage in things like self-harm, alcohol or excessive diet and exercise to help us cope. The ability to find some solace, respite or escapism in these activities helps us to escape or transport ourselves out of our own heads for a period, and this respite provides a short-term coping strategy away from our own thoughts. Some people will make claims that drinking a bottle of wine helps them to sleep or become less socially uncomfortable. Others may claim that overeating helps them to feel more comfortable in the chaos of life, and yet others may suggest that avoidance of social situations helps them to feel less overwhelmed. All of these explanations may well be true, but they are not healthy ways of coping, because they displace the origin of their stress and anxiety onto something else, and they engage in behaviours that offer short-term relief but often lead to bigger problems if utilised in the long term.

Let me give an example of a reassurance-seeking behaviour that will illustrate how some behaviours can be utilised to cope with short-term stressful situations.

The example involves a coping behaviour called 'displacement'. Displacement occurs when the person focuses on one innocuous aspect of their life and claims to not be too concerned with another more significant aspect. It is commonly observed at funerals or wakes, where the bereaved person becomes consumed with ensuring there is enough tea and sandwiches for everyone, as a means of temporarily escaping the magnitude of their recent loss. There was also a story I heard once about when the *Titanic* was sinking and one of the senior naval officers was observed to be rearranging the filing cabinet in his office. There were claims that he had lost his mind because he was engaging in this behaviour, but I would interpret it as his attempt to displace his anxieties into something he could control rather than spending time contemplating the possibility of plunging to almost certain death in the freezing ocean.

Displacement of anxiety happens all the time in less severe situations, so let me give an example to illustrate how it might occur.

A colleague of mine was new to a senior management position and there was an announcement that there was an independent audit team coming to do a review of the service. This was crunch time for my colleague, who was largely responsible for preparing the service for the review. Although an incredibly capable professional, this particular colleague had some doubts about his professional ability. I knew he must have been nervous about the imminent review, but he repeatedly claimed to be fine, often replying with remarks like 'It is what it is.'

However, there was one other unrelated issue that he seemed quite concerned about. He told me that he had pulled out of his parking spot that morning and noticed a stain on the ground. He told me he was concerned that there was an oil leak in his car. He knew I had a keen interest in cars and asked me to have a look at it. I thought an oil leak would be unlikely, as his car was relatively new, but I offered to have a look. I got under the car and looked all around and reassured him that there was no sign of any leak and that he should be fine. He thanked me and seemed reassured, and he went about the rest of his day.

Two days later, he said that he was still worried about the oil leak in his car and decided to take it to a mechanic to have a look at it. There were no more stains on his parking spot, but he claimed he was 'just uneasy about it' and wanted to get it looked at 'properly'. A few days later, he told me that the mechanic had not seen any sign of any oil leaks and he had repeated what I said to him. Once again, he said he felt relieved and was glad he had gone to the mechanic, as it had provided him with some 'peace of mind'.

Three days later, which was the day before the service review was about to happen, he said that he was still concerned about the oil leak. He said that the last mechanic he went to hadn't put his car up on a ramp, and while Googling oil leaks at home the previous night, he had read that a proper inspection for leaks would require a car to be placed on a ramp, so he was worried the mechanic hadn't inspected it properly. He told me he had rung around a few other mechanics that morning and had organised an appointment the following week with another mechanic who had committed to inspecting his car under a ramp. The service review was carried out the following day, and as expected the service passed with flying colours, with special mention of my colleague's contribution and his excellent work. The following week, I asked him how he had got on with the ramp inspection of his car and he replied that he had cancelled it because the more he thought about it the more he realised he was 'just being neurotic'.

This is a perfect example of displaced anxiety. My colleague could not do anything to control his anxiety about the pending service review. How that was going to go was out of his hands. But by mechanic shopping and Googling, he felt he was doing something useful and exerting some control over the suspected oil leak in his car. The illusion of action helped him to feel a sense of pseudo-control, and the multiple reassurances he got about the non-oil leaks offered him some temporary relief from his anxiety. But this was only short-lived, and only resulted in him seeking other more intense ways of receiving more reassurance. The meaning of his behaviour could be explained by the fact that his anxiety originated from the pending service review, and he felt overwhelmed. The function of his behaviour (visiting mechanics) was to offer him a series of gratifying reassurances that, though short-lived, did offer temporary relief. His behaviour wasn't the problem; it was a signpost to the problem. Once the review was passed and the origin of his stress was no longer there, the mechanic shopping became redundant, as he did not require reassurance anymore.

This is an everyday example of how stress and anxiety can get displaced from their place of origin onto something utterly random. It provides an illusion of control and allows the person to feel some sense of mastery or autonomy over something, even if is unrelated to the source of their stress. But the reassurance that started out as the solution behaviour soon became the problem behaviour. The interesting dynamic here is that once the service review was over, the need for reassurance was no longer there, highlighting the need to identify *why* someone is engaging in a certain behaviour rather than just measuring *how much* of the behaviour they are engaging in.

Control

The second function of some behaviours is control. When we feel overwhelmed by life circumstances that we feel we have no influence over, that feeling can cause us to desperately seek some control over something else in our lives. This is where rigid control over our food, weight or shape can temporarily provide us with compensation for the other aspects of our lives that we feel are overwhelming and unmanageable. This can be explained by preoccupation with the symptom. Obsessing over certain aspects of our lives can be an attempt to control our emotions and is often an attempt at trying to not become overwhelmed.

Let me explain.

We all have a finite amount of space in our minds to think about things. We therefore allocate a percentage of our thinking time to certain things. The illustration below explains how we apportion percentages of our thinking/feeling time to certain things. Let's imagine the white section is our family life, the light grey section is our friendships, the dark grey section is our financial situation, and the black section is our work.

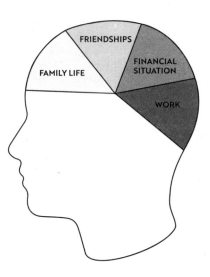

If we are going through a stressful period of our lives, our family relationships might be under pressure, our friendships might be tense and difficult or non-existent, and our financial circumstances might be precarious to the extent that we are struggling to manage. All of these three areas – family, friends and finances – are stressful and overwhelming, and we have no capacity to 'fix' or influence them. As a result, we may choose to obsessively throw ourselves into our work. This creates the following image.

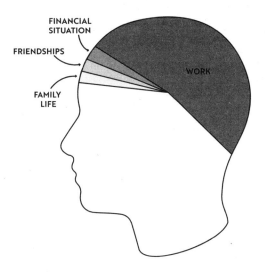

The difference in this image is that now the proportion of time we spend thinking/feeling about aspects of our lives has changed. In the first image we were spending 75 per cent of our time thinking/feeling about family, friends and finances – things that were overwhelming and that we felt we couldn't control – whereas in the second image we are now spending 90 per cent of our thinking/feeling time on work, which is something we feel we can influence or control. This dispro-portionate, obsessional or workaholic behaviour is a means of coping. It makes us feel less overwhelmed, as we feel we have more mastery over our lives. However, what is really happening is that we are achieving a sense of control over one aspect of our lives but neglecting to address the actual sources of our distress, which are the family, friends and finances aspects of our lives. This preoccupation with controllable variables may make us feel better in the short term, but it creates a longer-term problem.

We could replace the work section with alcohol, drugs, food restriction or fanatical exercise. These are all popular 'go-to' obsessional behaviours to achieve a short-term feeling of control, but they run the risk of creating a set of longer-term problems. This is why the 4–7 zone becomes so important. These behaviours tend to creep up on us without our noticing them. The gradual nature of our control-based behaviours means that we can justify them by saying that 'work is just really busy right now', or that 'I want to train for the marathon for my health', and these justifications can hide the fact that these are desperate attempts to regain a sense of control.

When we look at the second image, it is understandable to think that work is the problem area that needs to be addressed. In reality, though, it is the family, friends and finances aspects of our lives that are the origins of distress and therefore the areas of our lives that require attention in order to achieve long-term and sustainable change.

The 4–7 zone is a great tool to use to keep on top of our thinking/feelings and behaviours, because it requires us all to keep tabs on our functioning and highlights the areas that we are doing too much of – for example, work in the 8–10 zone – and the areas of our lives we may be neglecting – like our family relationships, friendships and finances in the 1–3 zone.

We can't avoid behaviours that are used to cope with emotional distress, but they need to come with a warning. A bit like a codeine-based painkiller, the advice is that you can use them to get over an acute phase of distress or emotional pain, but you shouldn't use them for too long or dependency can occur.

Communicate

The third function of problematic behaviour is communication. When we struggle to articulate in words how bad we feel, our behaviour becomes a clear indicator that all is not well and that we need some help. This communication is often quite obscure and sometimes can be contrary to what the person is saying they want. But if I am engaging in self-harm and someone discovers this inadvertently, it is a clear communication that I am not managing and I need some help.

The example I will describe to illustrate how behaviour can act as communication involves the actions of my son when he was only 14 months old, but it was a eureka moment for me and therefore worthy of sharing.

One Saturday morning, I placed my 14-month-old son up on the high chair and was all set to begin the messy process of feeding him breakfast. When I started to offer him the spoons of whatever baby rice had been left out for him, he began pushing the spoon away and holding his lips in a fashion that made them impressively airtight. This was not like him, as he had already established a reputation as someone who loved his food. I attempted the customary aeroplane motions and 'choo choo train' actions, but nothing worked. He maintained his position of refusal. I thought he might be ill, so I got the baby thermometer and placed it in his ear. Alas, he didn't have a temperature, so that didn't explain it. I decided that maybe he was just fed up with the baby rice and wanted something different. I made some toast, put lots of butter on it to make it nice and soft and offered this to him, but again he pushed the toast away and refused. I was running out of ideas, so I went off script and made him a bowl of Coco Pops. I thought, 'Every child loves chocolate-flavoured cereal. This will definitely work.' But to my amazement, the refusal extended even to the Coco Pops. As I sat there defeated, I noticed that he wasn't looking at me. His eyes were directed over my right shoulder. As I turned around to see what he was looking at, I noticed a Peppa Pig toy that was on a high shelf and seemed to be attracting his attention. I reached for the toy and gave it to him. Once he had the toy in his hand, he proceeded to eat the Coco Pops, the toast and the baby rice.

What this experience taught me was that his refusal was not about the food. He was trying to communicate to me that he needed or wanted something. Given his age, he did not have the language to articulate his desire, so his refusal was his way of communicating. The refusal was not 'I don't like your food', it was 'I want the Peppa Pig toy.' The 'problematic behaviour' was his way of communicating his needs to me.

I believe that many of us, despite our grasp of language, still use behaviours to communicate our needs. When language fails, behaviour takes over. It can be hard to communicate to those around us that we are lonely, stressed, not coping or in need of something. Being able to communicate our emotional needs is really difficult, even more so when we are adults and expected to be able to do it. Sometimes we all behave in ways that communicate on our behalf, because language is too difficult. Maybe it is embellishing a physical symptom to glean more sympathy. Maybe it is using alcohol in a way that creates concerns in others. Maybe it is losing weight to a level that makes others sit up and ask, 'Is everything OK?' We consider behavioural expressions as primarily the mechanism children use to garner attention, but as adults we are not immune to engaging in demonstrative behaviour to get the attention of those around us. Sulking, storming off or being unusually quiet is not purely limited to childhood, and these attempts to cope, control and communicate are common in adulthood too, although perhaps in a more sophisticated form.

Displacing emotional distress onto seemingly unrelated symptoms is not new. This can be observed in the history of mental illnesses. Back in the early 20th century, people who were admitted to psychiatric hospitals presented with very different concerns and presentations than people do nowadays. Back then, there were conditions like 'hysterical paralysis' and 'unexplained blindness'. There were no words for conditions like anxiety disorders or depression, so most people who were psychologically or emotionally distressed expressed it through symptoms in the body, which we would describe as 'psychosomatic symptoms'. Psychosomatic symptoms are currently mostly observed in children who develop things like recurrent abdominal pain in response to stress. This is because, like the people in the early 20th century, children do not have the words to express emotional distress, and so they too experience it in the body.

Sometimes we veer into the 1–3 and 8–10 zones as a means of letting those around us know that all is not well and that we need some help.

Reflection Exercise

It is really important that we are honest with ourselves when considering our own behaviours and what function they are serving. If we are finding an aspect of our lives is proving challenging or is being brought to our attention by others, it is important to privately ask ourselves if this could be a signpost to another more significant problem.

Am I working so much because I am trying to avoid being at home because of issues going on there?

Am I getting angry at my child's teacher for being unhelpful, when really I am concerned about my child's learning needs?

Am I testing my partner by being aloof around them because I feel invisible and I want them to ask me what's wrong?

Am I avoiding going out with friends, not because it's too much effort to get ready, but instead because I feel that they are moving on in their lives more than me and I feel bad?

These are difficult questions to ask ourselves, but they are often the most important ones when we are trying to uncover what feelings might be influencing our decision-making and behaviour. Applying the 4–7 zone to both our behaviours and our emotional responses to life events will serve as a useful indicator of the origins of our distress and inform how we might best respond to them. If you notice that you are having an 8–10 emotional response to a life event that does not warrant it, then it is useful to explore what possible emotional dynamics might be at play. Equally, if you have an apparent underreaction to a life event, in the 1–3 zone, there may also be an emotional dynamic at play that suggests displacement of emotion to another area of your life or avoidance behaviours. The 4–7 zone will identify the scale of your reactions to life events, and using an honest appraisal of your behaviour to explore its possible meaning will illuminate the area of your life where the most meaningful changes need to happen.

It is important to first try to understand the subtleties of behaviour and why we do what we do before jumping in with possible solutions. We are all socially constructed by our environment. Whether that's the influence of growing up in a family being referred to as 'the quiet one', 'the bright one', 'the funny one' or 'the black sheep of the family', or growing up in a community that has extreme political or religious views, all of these social constructions impact how we think about and feel about the world. These social dynamics also influence how we see ourselves and therefore have an impact on our developing personality.

GETTING WHAT YOU DESERVE

Given that we have established the significant influence our emotions can have on the subtleties of our behaviour, it is important to consider the factors that contribute to how we feel about events in our lives. One of the most potent emotions that influences how we experience both good and bad things that happen to us in our lives relates to what we believe we deserve. This core concept is socially influenced and something that we learn over the course of our life experiences. It relates to the health of the relationship we have with ourselves and can determine how we experience both positive and negative life experiences. It is important that the lens through which we believe we deserve good or bad things in our lives is within the 4–7 zone, because if it is within the 8–10 zone we may believe that we deserve the best of everything and create a risk of narcissism, whereas if it is in the 1–3 zone we may feel that we don't deserve good experiences, which prevents us from achieving any joy in our lives because we explain away our achievements as 'just lucky' or 'a fluke'. As with most things we have discussed so far, the following section will explain why somewhere in the 4–7 zone is where we need to be when it comes to what we believe we deserve.

I remember some years ago sitting in the barber's while my eldest son was getting his hair cut. His little sister, who was four years old, was with us too. The radio was playing, and a song came on that my daughter knew, so she jumped off the chair and began dancing in the middle of the room.

I remember thinking what a lovely stage of life it was to be in, where you have no shame or self-consciousness and you just get up and dance to the music you like because you want to. I remember then feeling sad, because I became aware that my daughter's self-belief and freedom to dance in such a carefree way would not last forever. I feared that the world would take that freedom from her and she would become a prisoner of her self-consciousness. Unfortunately, that fear has since transpired and my daughter, who is now 10 years old, would never dance in the middle of the barber's anymore – in fact, she now refuses to come with us when her brothers are getting their haircuts because she's too embarrassed to be in a barber's.

This self-consciousness is formative to our personalities and our understanding of ourselves and the world. Our value systems and core beliefs are eroded and influenced as we progress through life. Experiences tell us what we should behave like and not behave like in order to be accepted. We are conditioned to be self-conscious and avoid anything that would attract bad social attention. We are introduced to concepts like 'shame' and 'guilt', which are cornerstones of almost all conditions that compromise our mental well-being. This process informs what we believe we deserve, and this informs our responses and reactions to almost every experience of our lives. In many ways, we are not born to be critical of ourselves. Rather, the world around us teaches us to be that way by giving us experiences and interactions that enable criticism to take place and self-consciousness to develop.

Central to the process of developing self-consciousness is what we believe we deserve. The development of our understanding of what we deserve is crucial to our development of well-being. The concept of what we deserve is not an evidence-based belief system. It often evades objectivity and becomes incredibly subjective and open to the influence of others. If we have mostly good experiences, then that might shape our view of ourselves because we believe that we deserve good things. But if this is overdone, it runs the risk of developing into a form of entitlement. If we have mostly bad experiences or some very significant bad experiences, our understanding of what we deserve can be contaminated. In these instances, we believe that all the bad experiences in our lives are confirmation of what we believe we deserve. We dismiss good experiences, which create feelings of guilt because we believe we didn't deserve them, minimising their potential to shape our view of ourselves.

To not allow the concept of what you believe you deserve to drive your decisions and experiences, you need to challenge the social constructions you have chosen to believe and adopt as your own. It is here that we can use the 4–7 zone again to help us understand and manage the impact of our social experiences on our beliefs and value systems.

Some people who perhaps have had experiences of betrayal, loss or vulnerability will have a low opinion of what they deserve. We can observe their expectations of how well they deserve to be treated as being in the 1–3 zone. This soon becomes a self-fulfilling prophecy, as each negative experience is further 'proof' of what they deserve.

If someone has experienced betrayal, loss or disappointment, they are often left feeling vulnerable. When we are hurt and vulnerable, two usual responses can occur. Let's imagine a young man finds out his girlfriend has been unfaithful. He is distressed, upset and angry. His reactions will be largely limited to two responses. The first is that 'all women are bad and I am good', which offers him some short-term gratification, but which over time may morph into 'all women are good and I am bad'. This is where we begin to wonder if the betrayal was something to do with us and perhaps question whether we were not enough for the unfaithful person. Depending on the response, the person will either develop a cynicism around relationships and avoid engaging in any meaningful way in future relationships, or they will have the opposite response and try desperately to please any potential romantic partner.

Depending on our relationship with ourselves, our experiences of adversity can be interpreted differently. If an event causes a disproportionate reaction in us, it is worth stepping back and assessing that reaction. This applies in either extreme, whether you feel that the events that have just occurred are completely your fault and you are taking all the responsibility for them or you are convinced the events are completely everyone else's fault and you can take no responsibility for their occurrence. Of course, there are some events where there is a clear culprit and victim, but these are not all that common.

In most cases there are a myriad of factors that lead to events unfolding. The application of the 4–7 zone would require you to question any extreme emotional reactions that you may have after a life event and test the reliability of those assumptions.

Reflection Exercise

If you feel that you were totally at fault and you deserve for these bad things to happen to you, you may need to question that and ask yourself if the explanation could be less black and white, and instead maybe look for the grey. If you have a disagreement with a colleague about a communication issue that caused something to be missed, and you are blaming yourself completely for this incident and carrying all of the responsibility, step back and reflect on your reaction using the 4–7 zone as a guide.

Alternatively, if you feel that you are 100 per cent right and you have no responsibility for something happening, you should equally step back and try to honestly appraise the events that unfolded and once again look for the grey. Perhaps ask yourself if there was some part of the communication process that you were unclear about. If you had a chance to redo any aspect of the process, would you have done anything differently?

It is tempting to see things in the extreme because it spares us any ambiguity, but this process is most likely to be the work of the emotional mind, which is extreme and irrational. By inviting some honest reflection into the conversation with yourself and examining your reactions in the context of the 4–7 zone, you may be able to find that the situation is less clear than you initially thought, and a more measured response and understanding of the events might better inform what you believe you deserve. You may find out that what you thought you deserved was inaccurate, and this will help you to have a more balanced approach to the situation.

Our response to issues that occur in our lives can be on a spectrum of 'passive', 'assertive' and 'aggressive'. Some people will glorify aggressiveness as a show of strength and solidity and others will sometimes mistake agreeableness for likeability. By applying the 4–7 zone, we should be striving for the middle ground position of assertiveness that allows us not to be overlooked or passed over, but also avoids us being overly confrontational. While the consequences of being overly aggressive are well known, the issues that can arise from being overly agreeable are not.

I often see the shortcomings of agreeableness in my clinical work. Someone has had an experience of being bullied or mistreated, and when they enter into subsequent relationships, they are terrified of it happening again and adopt what I call the 'I don't mind' mindset. This approach is deemed to be safe and runs a low risk of causing any offence to anyone, and therefore the chances of getting rejected are perceived as low. However, what the 'I don't mind' mindset communicates is a lack of self-value and self-worth, which in reality leaves the person even more vulnerable to being overlooked or undermined. The self-fulfilling prophecy usually plays out and the person again ends up not being treated respectfully, which further compounds their low self-worth. As this is repeated, the belief that 'it must be something that is wrong with me' becomes the mindset, and so the belief emerges that 'this must be what I deserve', meaning the downward spiral of low self-value continues.

The 4–7 zone would help to break this downward spiral of self-worth, because it would argue against the 'I don't mind' mindset, which would be a 1–3 zone reaction, and it would also mitigate against the 'everyone is wrong and I am right' response, which would be an 8–10 reaction. The 4–7 zone would encourage the individual to experience the upset of the betrayal or loss, spend some time in the 1–3 zone and possibly interchange between this response and an 8–10 angry response. But this would be short-lived. By exercising the 4–7 zone, the person would be reminded to not spend too much time in the 1–3 or 8–10 zones and instead find their way to the measured 4–7 zone. This would lead to their engaging in future relationships with a degree of caution, for sure, but with a strong degree of self-value and self-respect, which would defend them from being overly vulnerable and permitting the cycle of low self-worth to continue.

As well as those people who experience low self-worth and believe they do not deserve anything, others may have an inflated sense of self-worth and function in an 8–10 zone of belief in what they deserve. They may have beliefs around their own 'specialness', and as a result believe they are never to blame for anything and that all of the negative things that happen in their lives are a result of the actions of others. What people like this believe they deserve is excessive and not proportionate, and oddly also leaves them vulnerable to disappointment.

To manage the impact of our experiences, we need to take the 4–7 approach, as this will shape our beliefs to move up from the 1–3 zone of feeling we are undeserving and down from the 8–10 zone of narcissism. We need to hold a mirror up to ourselves and question whether our responses to social experience verge on the entitled position of narcissism or the self-defeating position of feeling undeserving.

CONCLUSION

Creating an understanding of the 'function' of our behaviour and accompanying this with an awareness of the influence of our childhood experiences and temperament allows us to assign a 'why' to what we do. Understanding and knowledge do not guarantee change, but they may go a long way to explain why our previous attempts may not have worked. Attempting to challenge a personal behaviour without a clear understanding of its function, purpose and origin greatly diminishes our chances of success.

The benefits of establishing a meaning to explain our behaviour are significant. If we can address the origin of our difficulties, we are far more likely to achieve meaningful and lasting change. The process of stepping back is so obvious and simple, but it is probably the most neglected step when it comes to addressing problematic behaviours. The process of examining our emotional responses and trying to see these as important signposts to the origin of our upset encourages us to not jump straight in to eliminate the problem behaviour. Instead, it encourages us to take time to understand our motivations and reactions. With the aid of the 4–7 zone, we can improve our chances of responding to the cause instead of reacting to the symptom.

CHAPTER TWELVE

Establishing How Much is Enough and Creating Your Own Values

Now that we have established several reasons for why we may do what we do, we have a plan to not allow these actions to remain in the 8–10 or 1–3 zones for too long, dominating our lives. The final piece of advice to effectively implement the 4–7 zone is to establish your own personal sense of enough by creating more meaningful values. It is not my intention to tell you what values you need to have, as this is a subjective process, but I will try to get you to think about what values are important to you and how you can achieve contentment by establishing your own priorities and deciding how much is enough in your life. It is my view that good educators tell

someone where to look; they don't tell them what to see.
Therefore, the following is a series of suggestions that require
us all to examine who, and what, is influencing our expectations and values, and show us how to determine our own
needs and desires.

FINDING YOUR ENOUGH

Why is it so difficult to identify what values are important to us? I believe that our desires and our attention have
never been more manipulated than they are now. This has
created real difficulty in establishing what our individual values are and establishing how much of anything is
enough. Our values seem to be constantly under the scru-
tiny of other people and we are often called upon to defend
our values by those who may oppose or disagree with them.
From the humble brag of the school gate mothers who seem
affronted by the fact that your five-year-old cannot yet swim
to your classmates from your old school who are sharing yet
another work promotion on LinkedIn, there is undoubtedly
a pressure on everyone to be thriving, keeping all the plates
spinning and being all things to all people. We are also
constantly being told what we should value, and there seems
to be a belief that feeling satisfied is the same as 'settling',
which is apparently not good. But who is defining our values,
and are our actions a true reflection of our 'actual' values
or merely a performance of what we believe we are *supposed
to*, or *should* value?

I am always interested when people are asked about the best experience of their lives. Some seem to automatically go to the day their children were born. Or some will preface another example with 'Apart from obviously when my children were born, the next best day was …'. This is an example of prioritising what we think we *should* prioritise as opposed to what we might *want* to prioritise. As the father of three children, I can safely say that the arrivals of each of my children into the world were all very special days in my life, and of course there was a high level of emotional intensity on each occasion. Of course it is a lovely moment when you meet your child for the first time, but those were also difficult days that were stressful and tiring. I'm not sure that our experience of those moments is recalled through the influence of what we *actually* felt as opposed to what we think we *should* have felt.

I wonder if we mention those moments when we are asked to prioritise the highlights of our lives because we believe we should mention them rather than because we believe them to be true. There were other moments in my life that were also 'up there' in terms of specialness. Winning the Captain's Prize in the local golf society in 2009 was a great moment in my life. A night out with my friends in Tralee in 1999 was an awesome experience too. But I fear there would be harsh judgement of my priorities if I were to rate those memories over the births of my children, so if I am ever asked I will trot out 'when my kids were born' just to please everybody. This is an example of debating a choice between my thinking mind and my emotional mind, concluding that my emotional mind is correct, but nevertheless choosing to express the preference of my thinking mind so that my response is more acceptable. So, sometimes our priorities in life are determined by what we feel we *should* prioritise rather than what we feel we *want* to prioritise, which reminds me of the statement I hear repeatedly from clients: 'I have spent my whole life being whom I believed other people wanted me to be, and I forgot to be myself.'

The Pandemic of Discontent

The outside influences of culture make it hard to decipher what is important and what is not. As I began this book, I spoke about the surge in anxiety that seems to be ripping through our societies, and although we have definitely had lots of anxiety-provoking experiences in recent years, like the small matters of a global pandemic, climate crisis and conflict, it wasn't these that people were getting anxious about. Of course there was concern about these exceptional global events, but they were not what people were presenting to therapy for help with. Instead, it seemed to be a pandemic of discontent that was troubling most people. People worried about not being happy and were anxious that they weren't happy enough. There was an interesting dynamic that occurred where people were suggesting that they weren't *un*happy, but that there was a notable *absence of happiness* in their lives.

Many people were anxious about not being happy and then felt guilty for being so anxious when they couldn't explain why.

In his book *The Subtle Art of Not Giving a F*ck*, Mark Manson describes this as 'The Feedback Loop from Hell', which involves a feeling of anxiety that is unexplainable, and so we feel anxious and angry for feeling anxious, leading to an increase in our anxiety, and so the loop continues. This wave of discontent was not related to specific aspects of people's lives that were troublesome or 'going wrong'. In fact, many people who attended me for therapy would describe their lives as 'OK'. But when we drilled deeper into the situation, the reason they were unhappy was that 'OK' didn't feel like they were happy enough, which led to feelings of discontent.

This got me thinking about the concept of discontent. Many people who had much tougher lives than we do now will reflect on their childhoods with a degree of positive nostalgia. I do it myself. I reminisce about growing up in the 1980s and 1990s and recall the fun and carefree nature of my existence. I talk fondly of the summers when we went off as children for the day and only came home to be fed or to go to bed. I talk about fishing for newts in ponds with my friends and riding my BMX Burner up the country roads, with no hands on the handlebars, and thinking I was the coolest thing since sliced bread. However, back then we had far less than we do now.

The Tyranny of Choice

When I reflect on that time, I can see that it couldn't have been the utopian existence I remember at all. In the late 1980s and early 1990s there was little or no mental health awareness and there were no online banking facilities. We took photographs that we couldn't check immediately, so we had to hope that they would turn out OK when they eventually got developed a few weeks later. In 1980s Ireland, there was an economic recession. People were emigrating in their droves to the UK, Australia and the US. Northern Ireland was at the height of the Troubles, and there was news of bombings and shootings almost every day. While I appreciate that these things don't really impact children in the same way they do adults, which might explain my blind nostalgia for that era, it may also be related to the fact that I didn't know what I was missing. I believe that fewer choices brought with them less stress.

There was a TV show called *Bosco* on Irish television in the 1980s that was aimed at three- to six-year-olds. I watched *Bosco* until I was about 13 years old. This was not because I had some form of developmental delay; it was merely because it was the only thing that was on. Now I have Netflix, Prime, Apple TV and Disney+ and I spend more time browsing the menus of what to watch than I do actually watching anything. This is because the tyranny of choice, which was not a feature of life back in the 1980s and 1990s, means that the more options available for us to choose from the more anxious we become. With more choice, our sense of enough moves.

We don't miss what we never had, and in hindsight I don't know how we survived with no internet, Wi-Fi, smartphones or Netflix back then. While I might claim they were simpler times, if I had the choice I would not go back there now, as I am someone who has travelled over 40km back to my house to pick up my phone when I had forgotten it, rather than try to survive a day without it. So, is it the dynamic of nostalgia that makes us remember our childhood with rose-tinted glasses, or was it 'better' back then? Because despite the option to return to aspects of that time in my life now, I don't do it. It is not so much that I don't want my life to be simpler; it is that modern-day life would not accommodate that way of living. We have become dependent on our life-assistive technologies now, and the easier things become, the harder the easier things appear.

For me, this dynamic is relative to our expectations rather than our realities. Perhaps the gap between expectation and reality wasn't as wide in the 1980s as it is now. It is my view that what has happened in recent decades is that our expectations have risen to the extent that we do not feel we should ever be bored or have to wait for anything – or, God forbid, ever use our time suboptimally. As a result, we have lost all sense of the concept of enough, and this hasn't happened because our realities are any worse than they were back then, but because our subjective expectations of what is enough have increased substantially.

'Enough': Wants, Needs, Expectations and Requirements

We hear the term 'good enough' a lot within the field of psychology and self-help, but what does it actually mean? The definition of 'enough' is simply 'as much as is required'. This means that it is a subjective concept, because it depends completely on what the requirement is. For example, two wheels are enough for a bicycle, but they wouldn't be enough for a car to function. Therefore, it is up to us to establish how much we 'require', and this will in turn define our enough. But there is a difference between what we require and what we desire, and this complicates matters considerably. So, we may require food, shelter and company, but that minimum requirement would not satisfy the desires of a lot of people. Therefore, rather than focus on what we need, we must look at what we want, and how that is influenced considerably by our culture and environment.

One of the major issues that causes us to struggle with desire, expectation and enough is the conflation of 'wants' and 'needs'. Our culture is dominated by this dynamic. Advertisers are convincing us all the time that we need things that we want. An inability to distinguish between these concepts is core to our polarised and extreme views of our lives and ourselves. If we are being convinced by advertisers selling products or peers selling notions, then we are going to become consumed with expectation. Our expectations of ourselves, our lives and our families are being constantly inflated by the dynamic of comparison, and this is having an impact on our sense of self, leaving us feeling disenfranchised and in a state of constant discontent.

The polarisation of our views is also important to our understanding of this dynamic. We are viewing experiences and life events in very extreme, black and white ways, and the idea of considering life experiences on a continuum or spectrum has become unpopular. In reality, however, very few experiences in life are clear-cut. The fantasy of a black and white world is just that – a fantasy. The reality is that most aspects of life are decidedly 'grey'. This is why we need to view our world and ourselves in a way that accommodates fluctuation and a variety of outcomes.

If we consider needs and wants as a spectrum, we can see clearly how we might 'need' food, shelter, love and safety, and 'want' success, materialistic items and popularity. But there are a whole other set of experiences between these poles that merit consideration. Our expectations are often what set the tone for where we situate ourselves on this spectrum, but our expectations are open to manipulation and contamination by others and may need to be challenged. With this in mind, it may be useful to incorporate another lens with which to interpret this continuum: the lens of 'requirements'. This would allow us to delineate between 'wants' and 'needs' and set our own goals for what we consider to be enough without this being influenced by expectations.

For many, shelter, love and safety may not be enough, and this is not unreasonable. Perhaps we *should* hope and aim for more than just survival, but how then can we taper our expectations of ourselves to avoid being swept up in the allure of the hypercomparative world of endless desire? Maybe the key to this is establishing an understanding of our requirements and allowing these to extend beyond things like achievement, accolades or status.

Perhaps it is simply contentment, authenticity and realness that we require. Perhaps we require a degree of satisfaction that makes us feel like our efforts are valuable, or a sense of meaning in our relationships. And perhaps it is our requirements rather than our expectations that should drive our actions. If we can consolidate the idea that our requirements are driven by our own goals and not contaminated by the expectations of others, we are far more likely to achieve a more content experience in our lives.

Requirements fit neatly within the principles of the 4–7 zone. Requirements are set by the individual, not the environment. They ground us in our actual value systems and spare us from chasing the values of others. If we consider our needs and wants on a continuum, perhaps our needs are 1–3 and our wants/desires are 8–10, leaving our requirements in the 4–7 zone. This would mean that it is OK to just survive from time to time – life will throw us curveballs where simply meeting our needs is all we can do. It is also OK to seek out our desires and wants – at times in our lives we may well be on the crest of a wave and experience all we hoped for. But this too will pass, and we will return to periods in our lives where we have what we require, and that is OK. We need to become content with having what we require, as what we require is enough.

This brings us to the concept of desire, which is important in determining our mental well-being. The absence of desire in our lives can result in catastrophic events like suicide, and desire is crucial for us to function. Desire gets us out of bed in the morning, gets us to work on time and motivates us to do things. Motivation can be boiled down to two concepts, desire and fear, which are primary motivators for behaviour. So, to have a purpose we need to desire. But like most things, desire exists on a spectrum. We have a range of desires from 1–10 too. A lack of desire can lead to low motivation, apathy and indifference, which might be in the 1–3 zone. By contrast, an overzealous desire can be overwhelming and obsessive and exist in the 8–10 zone. In the spirit of the 4–7 zone, our desire is best placed somewhere in the middle so that it is sufficient to allow us to have function and purpose, but not so extreme that it consumes us and determines our values.

So, what is the current problem with desire, and how does it impact our sense of enough? It is very easy for desire to be manipulated. It can be stoked by experiences and events in our lives, and external events can act as catalysts in the context of desires. I may not have any desire for something to eat, but if someone enters the room with a bag of chips and the smell of salt and vinegar hits me, I may then become consumed with the desire for some greasy chipper food. Advertisers have built their whole industry on manipulating people's desires. We see an image of someone enjoying a food product or looking amazing after using a cosmetic or health product, and it triggers our desire to be like that. Our brains receive a message telling us we need that product and we should go and get it. Some people believe that this occurs in the thinking brain, but it also has an impact on and interaction with the emotional brain. Many of the most effective and memorable advertisements are ones that create feelings in the viewer, not just thoughts about the product. So, desire is not just a cognitive process; it is an emotional one.

For me, an understanding of how our desire can be manipulated has never been more important than it is now. With the pervasive nature of modern-day media, our desires are constantly manipulated and cultivated. And this is more powerful now than in the past because it is no longer only the huge advertising companies that are provoking our desires; it is also our peers. Previously, we might have seen an advertisement on the television for a furniture company selling a beautiful sofa and thought that it would be nice to have that sofa. Now we go on Instagram and see our neighbours, friends or family members displaying their new sofa, and it has a far deeper reach in terms of its impact. This is not so 'distant'; this is close. The closeness of the relationship heightens the intensity of the social comparison. Not only are we filled with thoughts, but we are impacted by feelings and emotions. These could be feelings of envy, anger or upset. We think, 'Why don't we have enough money for a new sofa?' Perhaps this makes us feel like we are getting something wrong, and creates expectations and desires that otherwise would not exist. It can extend beyond 'products' or 'things' to include other areas of our lives too.

If you are a parent, you may be familiar with the experience of going on a social media site and seeing a post from a friend about how their eight-year-old has just achieved a black belt in karate, and then you reflect on the fact that your eight-year-old still cannot tie their shoelaces. This again stirs up feelings of failure and alters your sense of enough. Instead of worrying about why your child can't tie their shoelaces, you forget to remember that your child is happy. They are getting on fine without a black belt in karate or getting a 'student of the week award' every other week. We are drawn to the areas of our lives that do not seem as 'full' as other people's lives, which can make us feel quite empty or 'not enough'.

I am always struck by how people concentrate on accolades and external variables rather than internal ones when they discuss their children: 'How is Mark doing?' 'Oh, Mark is great. He was delighted with his Junior Cert results, and he's captain of the soccer team and he's got a part-time job for the summer.' I long for the day when that conversation might go, 'How is Mark doing?' 'Oh, Mark is great. He has good friends and he's developing into a very kind young man, and he's no trouble, thankfully.' If we do not consider the internal variables to be important, we will dismiss them as superfluous, so we need to move the dial on our priorities and our understanding of enough.

So how do we decide how much is enough? How do we achieve contentment? I believe we do it by managing our expectations and reprioritising what we believe is important to us. This is where the 4–7 zone again comes into play. We need to realign our values to be more mature. We need to rise above our sofa envy and allow ourselves to determine what is enough for us. We are all blessed with the power of choice, which allows us to choose what we deem to be important. The difficult part of this is being able to drown out the white noise of comparison and find our own values.

CHOOSING GOOD VALUES

Our sense of enough may well be guided primarily by our values. How we prioritise our values will determine what aspects of our lives and ourselves need to be enough, and this will vary from person to person.

A value is a belief or attitude we hold to be good, and our value system is the set of values we wish to live by. This sounds fairly straightforward, but values are one of the most commonly misunderstood aspects of the 'self'.

It is my view that our values should be judged by our actions more than by our words. There are some 'popular' values that seem altruistic and noble, but which are not evident in our everyday behaviours. Many people will proclaim that their values are built around their health, family and friends, yet this is not clearly evident in their behaviours, as they appear to work almost 70 hours a week, have little or no time for friends and family, and seem primarily motivated by their job and financial security. This is not a judgement of a person's values; it is merely an observation.

Our values are influenced by many things such as our experiences, our environment and our sense of purpose and meaning, and they are accurately observed in how we spend our time. Time is a non-renewable resource and is something that we become consumed with for most of our lives. Many of us are preoccupied with 'using our time well' and become terrified of 'wasting time' on something. Our environment and culture often influence our understanding of the usefulness of time. There is a recent phenomenon that celebrates and glorifies being 'busy'. This tends to communicate that we are doing something useful with our time and not wasting it. If you value one thing over another, then you will more than likely observe that this will be where the bulk of your time is spent. Take the case of Jim in Chapter Five, who valued a conflict-free life more than he valued his own well-being. This was not something that was apparent to Jim at the time, because he, like most others, believed his values to be family, friends and health. In reality, his actions suggested quite the opposite.

Creating Our Own Values in Spite of Value Systems

The value systems that are lauded by a culture or society are powerful influences, greatly impacting our thoughts, feelings and actions. A culture that values 'success' will often determine what success looks like, and by default will allocate an understanding of what failure looks like. Does having a good job, a large income and an impressive life mean success, or does being content within your own circumstances reflect success? True autonomy occurs when we are able to step back and realign our values according to our own individual preferences, rather than being swept up in the value systems of our culture.

It is also important to see values as a moving target that shifts and changes according to our circumstances. My values in my mid-forties are very different from the values I had in my twenties. We need to take a step back periodically to review our values and question whether they are authentic and individual or overly determined by the culture around us or the need to perform altruistically.

This process of reorganising our hierarchy of values is an indicator of the personal growth and maturity of each individual. It is hoped that over time and after numerous life experiences, we begin to value effort over outcome and invest in fulfilment over gratification. We learn to re-establish and refine our value systems to represent fewer materialistic or pleasure-seeking values and more substantial, nourishing and fulfilling ones.

'Values' are more effective than 'rules'. Rules demand compliance, whereas values require 'buy-in' and therefore create more understanding and have a longer-term influence. It is unrealistic to expect someone in their early twenties to have a full long-term understanding of the need for a pension or a 10-year plan. These are unrealistic expectations and serve only as a route to becoming disappointed in ourselves. Our values in our early twenties are not supposed to include such long-term considerations, and so accepting this to be the case and allowing the more sensible values to emerge in time is a more effective approach.

Social Comparison and the Modern World

Having realistic and reasonable value systems has become ever more difficult in the modern world. Feedback, overexposure and the persecution of comparison all tell us that we need to have and be the best of everything. This is utterly unreasonable and can leave us feeling that we are 'losing at life' when we compare our lives with the seemingly impressive highlight reels of others.

It is my view that the world of social media – in addition to compounding the idea that comparison is the thief of joy – has negatively impacted our collective maturity. At the risk of sounding snobbish or superior, social media platforms like TikTok are by definition immature. What has occurred is that the culture of social media has dragged whole cohorts of people of all ages into immature means of communication. I don't mean this as a judgement against people in their fifties who make TikTok dance videos. Rather, I am referring to the juvenile exchanges, such as name-calling, that can be observed on platforms like Twitter.

When we step back from the technology narrative, the immaturity of our involvement and activity on these platforms is sobering. We have been enticed into a world of validation and recognition that feeds our egos only to make us feel more inadequate. Despite knowing that this is the case, we continue to do it.

Social comparison is unavoidable, as many people find it functional to compare themselves with others who have similar attributes. This process has always been central to our definition of the 'self'. But the online environment is filled with pictures of peers and opportunities for social comparisons, and negative comparisons become particularly likely when users do not acknowledge that their peers' photos have been carefully selected and digitally altered.

Our exposure to content in our environment influences our values and expectations via the feedback loop spiral. This is where we are guided towards appearance-focused social media content that can lead to users seeking particular gratifications, such as reassurance and validation. These gratifications propel us to spend considerably more time on this content, triggering a host of psychological processes. Continued use then leads to increased life dissatisfaction and negative affective reactions, and a feedback loop ensues. We are then even more motivated to alleviate this negative feeling, so we seek even more validation, thereby exposing ourselves to online comparison yet again.

For example, we begin by simply browsing through pictures of others who are more attractive and less attractive than us, and this causes us to engage in upward and downward comparisons. This can then cause us to ruminate about parts of our lives we are unhappy about and leave us feeling unhappy and dissatisfied. The only apparent response to this is to bolster our own self-worth by seeking out others with whom we can make downward comparisons, only to come across others we deem even more impressive, and so the slot machine of validation continues.

We can all be critical of those I have described in the paragraphs above, but the reality is that to some degree or another these dynamics impact all of us. The influence of the dynamic of social comparison and how we can get seduced into it unbeknownst to ourselves is illustrated in the following example:

Imagine you are a mother helping your nine-year-old child with a school project. You assist them in writing out some words on a page, cutting out pictures from a magazine and sticking them onto it. You may be satisfied with this.

However, while at the school gate you hear some of the other parents describe how they helped their child complete a PowerPoint presentation and make 3-D models as part of their project. Now your opinion has changed. Maybe what you thought was 'enough' is now 'not enough'.

Despite telling yourself that this is ridiculous, you don't want to be the parent who sends their child to class with a crappy project. Your expectations then move upward, and this creates pressure. You possibly try to improve your child's project, but you cannot compete with the PowerPoint presentations and the

3-D models. As you see the other mothers share images of their child's amazing projects on Instagram and the energised discussions on the parents' WhatsApp group detailing how much they are loving doing the project with their child and how much they are enjoying the process, you feel like a bad parent.

This feeling has an impact on your expectations of yourself and begins a negative feedback loop. If you are the bad parent when it comes to school projects, does that mean you are bad at everything else too? Is your child suffering as a result of your laziness? You may think that you need to invest more time in your child's homework and invest more money in their education in order to keep up with everyone else. But when you assess your life, you cannot work out where you are going to find the time to put this effort in, as you work full-time and you are already stretched as it is.

As the school projects get bigger and more advanced and the birthday parties become more extravagant, the expectations that you put on yourself continue to rise. Despite your best efforts, you cannot keep up with the other parents, who perhaps have bigger incomes and are not working full-time. Your reality doesn't change. You cannot put in more hours in the week. Despite trying so hard, you still feel like you are falling short. No matter how hard you try, your efforts don't seem to be enough. The gap between your expectation of yourself as a parent and the reality of your parenting performance is big. This gap is the amount of anxiety, upset and disgruntlement that you are able to feel. Your relationship with yourself deteriorates. You feel like you are not enough. This makes you feel worried, sad and like you are failing.

This is just a simple example of how our expectations of ourselves can be manipulated, despite our best efforts. The crux of the problem for this mother is that her value system was dictated to her by other people. She wasn't investing time and energy into the school project because she believed it was a worthwhile investment in her child's learning, she was doing it because she didn't want her child to be left behind. The pressure she was putting on herself was applied by other people. Her anxiety and expectations were being driven into the 8–10 zone by the other parents. As a consequence, her self-worth and evaluation of her parenting were plummeting into the 1–3 zone. This is largely unavoidable when we are faced with these types of situations, but by applying the 4–7 zone she may be able to gain a sense of perspective over the situation. Stepping back and asking herself why she is allowing herself to be polarised by these experiences may allow her to regain some context.

After realising her stress is in the 8–10 zone and her self-worth is in the 1–3 zone, she must ask herself what good this is doing for her child's longer-term sense of well-being. By witnessing his mother become so distressed about a school project, what message and what value system is she communicating to her nine-year-old son?

By grounding herself in her own values and implementing the 4–7 zone, this mother would be able to resist the urge to get swept up in the madness. Of course, there is the short-term risk that her child's project will not be as 'impressive' as the others, but she may realise that the problem is not her lack of effort; rather, the problem is the other parents' over-the-top efforts. If other people want to overvalue a task and overinvest in it, let them. That does not mean that we need to do the same.

Reflection Exercise

Remember, 'enough' is a subjective concept that you define for yourself. Don't let other people define your enough. If you do, you consign yourself to a life of disappointment and the feeling that you have fallen short.

When those around you are living in the 8–10 and 1–3 zones, leave them at it. Don't follow them in there. You are privileged with the capacity to choose, and it is our choices that define us, not our circumstances. By staying grounded amid the swell of hype, you allow yourself to make better choices. By reminding yourself of your own values, you will make better choices. By tapering your expectations of yourself, you will make better choices.

The choices we make will determine where we focus our efforts, energy and attention. There are so many influences trying to sway our choices that we are constantly having to put an effort into not getting carried away by them. It is my belief that the 4–7 zone will help you to hold onto that grounding, protect you from being swept up in a swell of expectation, and by default improve your decisions, your priorities and your life.

Here is a practical exercise that will help you work out what you truly value in life. As an experiment, consider the list below and select between two and four values that are completely determined by you. Before selecting your choices, remove all pressure from others from your mind. Choose the values that are closest to your desires and are not contaminated by the influence of others.

Authenticity	Expression	Respect
Accountability	Gratitude	Safety
Adventure	Growth	Security
Ambition	Health	Spirituality
Belonging	Hope	Success
Confidence	Independence	Time
Contentment	Joy	Truth
Courage	Knowledge	Understanding
Curiosity	Peace	Uniqueness
Dignity	Power	Wealth
Environment	Pride	Wisdom
Equality	Reliability	

Ask yourself what percentage of your daily behaviours, actions and thoughts are aligned with the values you have selected. If there is a small percentage, then you need to initiate some changes. One of the most protective aspects of our mental well-being is the ability to be authentic and real. The relief inherent in being able to 'be yourself' is often palpable, and we only realise the stress and pressure of performance when we are relieved of the need to do it. So many of our actions, thoughts and feelings are built upon our values, and being true to these values can allow us to genuinely nurture our self-worth, self-value and self-belief. Remember that being applauded for performance is far less impactful than being appreciated for who you are, and this is why the 4–7 zone is a great guide towards authenticity. When we remove the pressure and expectation to be exceptional, we can achieve a greater degree of self-acceptance.

This is why I believe the 4–7 zone is so important in today's world. In a world that celebrates excess and normalises it, we have lost all sense of enough. This loss of enough is playing a huge role in our well-being issues. With no enough, there can be no contentment. Therefore, we need to challenge the value systems being promoted by the world of technology, take control of choosing our values and try desperately hard to create a sense of enough. It is my view that our core beliefs and value systems are where our concept of 'enough' is established and exists. Therefore, it may not be down to us trying to regulate the world or online industries; it is about being able to regulate ourselves. The excuse of every online corporation is that they are 'just a platform' and it is the 'user' who is responsible for the content that is posted on their sites. Rather than continue to argue for their responsibilities to the user, let's try to take back the responsibility ourselves. It is time for us to collectively cease being bystanders and begin to become upstanding when it comes to reclaiming our own value systems. This may require us to take a step back, reassess the external influences and re-establish our own autonomy over our own choices, and this is where I believe the 4–7 zone is so important.

The 4–7 zone asks us to critique our value systems and identify what influences them. It encourages us to examine how extreme our views, beliefs, actions and feelings are around certain aspects of our lives and to ask ourselves if they are the views, beliefs, actions and feelings we want in our lives. If not, we are encouraged to explore what and who is influencing our value systems and how we can retake control over our choices. The 4–7 zone also asks us to be aware of how extreme our views, beliefs, actions and feelings have become, and to be upfront about how long they have been that way.

CHAPTER THIRTEEN

Becoming Your Own Therapist

With the demand for psychological support services being what they are, there is a high likelihood that if we require some psychological support, we will have to wait for it. The waiting times can vary according to the catchment area, postcode lottery, what services exist in your locality, or the financial resources at your disposal. No matter what the circumstances, it might be a good idea to know what to do in the meantime.

Remembering that all sadness is not depression and all worry is not anxiety, it is important to try to assess your emotional experiences and see if they are what could be described as 'proportionate' reactions to life circumstances. This entails exploring the full breadth of your experiences and trying to honestly identify circumstances that may be causing you emotional discomfort.

Emotions are not 'bad things'. Even uncomfortable or difficult emotions are not always bad. Much like physical pain is the
body's way of communicating that there is something 'wrong'
inside the body, so emotional pain is a similar process for the
mind. The discomfort we feel is indicative of pain or discomfort
in our emotional lives that requires our attention. Sometimes
this can be less obvious – for example, when our stress is being
communicated through a physical symptom such as stomach
cramps or neck pain – but it is communication nonetheless
and requires us to pay heed to it. The emotional pain of sadness
may be the result of the loss of a relationship or a difficult life
experience, and this emotional pain is warning us that we are
struggling internally with something.

It is important that we have some understanding of what is
going on and how these events in our lives have impacted on us,
but the understanding of recovery is almost more important.
Sometimes we feel that we must 'rid' ourselves of our negative life experiences. There is a fantasy that we can turn back
time and redo something that has been done, or we can return
to the lost relationship and fix it. In many instances, this is
not possible. We cannot 'undo', 'unsee' or 'unfeel' something.
These experiences have happened and there is no removing
their existence.

There is, however, a potential to readdress the impact
of these experiences on our ongoing lives. There is a way of
reframing these experiences to limit their impact on the lens
through which we see the world. Someone once said that

'the only things that can upset us are our memories and our imaginations'. When you think about it, that's true. How we recall the importance of something will determine how catastrophically we react to its loss. And how we imagine our lives will be affected by the loss or change of circumstances will influence the interpretation we have of the potential impact of the event on the rest of our lives. By managing and working on our memories and imaginations, we can greatly alter the potential impact of any event on our emotional well-being.

I often explain to people that sometimes life is like a glass of cordial, with the cordial representing the difficult experiences in our lives and the water being the good or hopeful ones. It is important to recognise that we cannot remove the cordial once it has been mixed. The bad experiences have happened, and we cannot undo them. So sometimes the only solution is to dilute the cordial as best we can by adding more water. Maximising the experiences that make us feel good, respected and wanted can and will minimise the toxicity of exclusion, betrayal and disappointment. The drive can sometimes be to undo the intensity of the past that has left our mood, hope and optimism in the 1–3 zone and our anxiety, fear and suspiciousness in the 8–10 zone. But by adding more experiences of joy, fun and hope into our lives, these corrective emotional experiences can move the dial towards the middle. As we have more affirming real-life experiences, our mood, hope and optimism will improve, and simultaneously our anxiety, fear and suspiciousness will reduce.

Many people believe that the change of perspective or the recovery from emotional pain occurs in the therapy room, but in many ways nothing could be further from the truth. In all my years of providing therapy to people, I have never witnessed someone recover in real time, or sitting in front of me. Yes, I have witnessed someone recover over time and I have observed how they have gone from strength to strength session after session, and the catalyst for that change may well be the therapy sessions, but the actual mechanics of recovery happen in between the sessions.

I have always thought psychotherapy to be like a physiotherapy process for emotions. If you had an injury to your knee and you received all the deep tissue massages in the world, it would not bring about any real change if you didn't do the exercises in between the sessions and take the brave initiative to start to walk. Similarly, the bravery of my clients is not disclosing details in a therapy session. Rather, it is taking on some advice and bravely executing it under very challenging real-life circumstances. The adult woman who finds the courage to stand up to her hypercritical mother, the person who takes a chance on making a radical change in their life and tolerates the vulnerability and uncertainty of it, the brave young man who leaves a relationship that is not good for him despite his crippling fears of being alone, or the woman who joins a local book club as a last-ditch attempt to address her sense of loneliness – these are not therapeutic interventions; they are brave life decisions. Change does not occur in the therapy room; it occurs in our lives. Therapy can play an important role in providing us with the encouragement and support to take on these changes, but it cannot do it for us.

In order to become your own therapist, you have to work on putting the challenges you face into perspective and try to meaningfully invest in nourishing your self-worth. If stress and anxiety make us overestimate the challenge and underestimate our own ability, then becoming your own therapist involves trying to counter that, not only through words and mantras, but through lived experiences.

PRACTICALLY IMPLEMENTING THE 4–7 ZONE IN YOUR LIFE

Hopefully by this point you have a better understanding of why I believe we need to integrate the 4–7 zone into our lives. The manner in which our lives have changed in the last decade has meant that there has been a significant impact on our expectations of life. The impact of advertising on our desires is not new, but the advances in our means of communication have meant that the capacity for the manipulation of our desire is much greater. This is why we need to institute countermeasures to stay grounded in our own values as opposed to getting swept up in the pervasive value systems that surround us.

The 4–7 zone is an important tool to allow us to regularly and periodically review our thoughts, feelings and behaviours so that we can identify when we are starting to lose our focus on what is important. The 4–7 zone is not a foolproof way of living our lives; rather, it is a technique for us to use to protect ourselves when we inevitably drift off course.

I see the 4–7 zone as similar to the speed limit signs that give us live feedback as to the speed we are doing. Many of us will be aware of the speed limits in certain areas, as they are well signposted along the route. But knowledge is a very small component of behavioural change, and although we know the speed limit, many of us will exceed it unwittingly. However, when we receive the feedback from the interactive sign telling us we are exceeding the regulated limit, we are more likely to slow down as a response. The 4–7 zone is a similar mechanism, as it assumes that we will all enter the 1–3 or 8–10 zones from time to time, or over- or underreact to events in our lives periodically and almost certainly get swept up in the pervasive culture of unrealistic expectation. But implementing the 4–7 zone using the six criteria for a mental health check will allow us to take stock so that we can realign our behaviours, challenge our thinking and improve our emotional well-being.

The idea that we are already under so much pressure to perform, excel and thrive is real, and I have no intention for the 4–7 zone to add to our already unrealistic expectations. Its purpose is not to add to the already overloaded list of things we 'need to do'. Instead, the 4–7 zone is a forgiving intervention that has the sole purpose of providing support to us when we are struggling and should complement our lives as opposed to adding to our challenges. That is why I have repeatedly stated that we will all find ourselves in the 1–3 and 8–10 zones from time to time. That is not only acceptable; it is inevitable. The 4-7 zone is a mechanism to help us to identify these inevitable slips and prompt us to keep them as brief as possible so that they do not create bigger problems over time.

The core message of the 4-7 zone is that early intervention is key to resolving problems. There are many areas of mental health and well-being where very little is known, but one thing that is beyond doubt is that when mental distress occurs, early intervention is key. We are all aware that the demand for mental health services is huge and there are delays in accessing support promptly. But the purpose of the 4-7 zone is to provide us with both a first-aid tool for early signs of mental distress and a low-maintenance way of maintaining our mental fitness. Similar to how our smartwatches prompt us to get up and move when we have been sitting too long, the 4-7 zone prompts us to do something small regularly to ensure we are maintaining our mental fitness. It's not demanding that we do the equivalent of a marathon, but more like a gentle nudge to take a small walk when we need to engage in some healthy movement.

The principle of the 4-7 zone is that it is often not the acuteness of our mental distress that determines its outcome but the longevity of its presence. That is why if we can manage to incorporate the 4-7 zone into our daily lives it will notify us that we are perhaps engaging in something unhelpful, and that if we do not do something to change things, it will develop into a more significant problem. Another aspect of the 4-7 zone is that we do not need to wait until we feel better to do something; instead, we should do something and then we will feel better. This message is central to the 4–7 zone philosophy and something to be mindful of as we integrate it into our lives.

Another important aspect of the 4–7 zone is that it is not a distraction-based technique. There are issues that arise in our lives that we cannot meditate through, and so the 4–7 zone asks us to step back and look at our behaviour and thinking and try to challenge any unhelpful aspects of those parts of our lives. If we notice that we are doing or thinking something too much and identify that these dimensions are in the 1–3 or 8–10 zones for a sustained period of time, we need to try to activate some change to address these patterns before they develop into more insurmountable challenges.

One of my favourite mantras is that 'failure is not falling down; it is refusing to get back up'. The reason I like this message is that it allows us to fail and explains that sometimes failure is not our fault. However, it does not negate the fact that how we respond to failures and disappointments is our responsibility. Even though we are not at fault, we still have a responsibility to react and respond to life events. The 4–7 zone is not about not getting lost in the woods of life. It is about admitting that we are lost and actively trying to find a way out.

Finally, it is important to acknowledge when the 4–7 zone is not enough and you need more. While the crux of this book is that it is a 'self-help tool', one of the most important aspects of any self-help strategy is noticing when you need an 'other-help' strategy. No technique, strategy or guide is capable of managing all of life's challenges. There are limits to our resilience, strength and robustness. When a problem is too big for us to manage, despite using every resource we have, the bravest step to take is to ask for help from someone else.

One of the greatest challenges is identifying when we should ask for help, and my response to that is that when you have tried everything at your disposal and it has not had the impact that you had hoped, then you need to reach out. The 4–7 zone will help us to maintain our mental fitness, but even the fittest people in the world get injured, and there is no shame in that. There is a myth that people who lack resilience end up in therapy or seeking emotional support, but in my experience nothing could be further from the truth. Some of the strongest people I have ever met have been sitting across from me in my therapy room, and every strategy and technique that I have evolved has come from them. The 4–7 zone is not something I plucked out of the sky. It is an approach that was developed and refined by observing how some of the most remarkable and courageous people overcame some of the most difficult challenges imaginable. That is why I am grateful to have accompanied them on their journeys and I am deeply appreciative of the lessons I have learned from them all.

That is why I have decided to share the 4–7 zone with you all. It has been a great help to me in my personal life and continues to help me to navigate life's challenges to this day. It has been something for which I have repeatedly received positive feedback from my clients, with some still quoting it many years after it was introduced to them.

I hope that you find that the 4–7 zone assists you in navigating your life's challenges and helps you to stay grounded in your own values, but always to maintain a degree of self-compassion as you go. Sometimes we are not failing at anything. Instead, we are surviving everything.

Mental Health Check

I will leave you with a tool that we can all fill out or consult from time to time in our lives. This short exercise will allow us to ground ourselves in our authentic value system and provide us with a means of checking in on our perspective. I would advise everyone to set a monthly reminder on their phone to complete this mental health check and see where they are at in terms of their needs, wants and requirements. I believe that this will allow us all to become our own therapists and serve as a helpful reminder that Reality − Expectation = Happiness, and while we cannot always change reality, we can always adjust our expectations.

Rate the following out of 10 to complete your mental health check.

DIMENSION	SCORE OUT OF 10	REASON FOR RATING	AMOUNT OF TIME IT HAS EXISTED	ACTION NEEDED
Behaviour				
Sleep				
Diet				
Exercise				
Alcohol				
Cognition				
Memory				
Concentration				
Negativity				
Positivity				

DIMENSION	SCORE OUT OF 10	REASON FOR RATING	AMOUNT OF TIME IT HAS EXISTED	ACTION NEEDED
Emotions				
Worry				
Sadness				
Joy				
Anger				
Frustration				
Loneliness				
Biology				
Energy Levels				
Stress Levels				
Nutrition				

DIMENSION	SCORE OUT OF 10	REASON FOR RATING	AMOUNT OF TIME IT HAS EXISTED	ACTION NEEDED
Psychology				
Optimism				
Hope				
Pessimism				
Social				
Friends				
Intimate Relationships				
Family				

Acknowledgements

While I am undoubtedly grateful to the team at Gill Books for their belief in me and their support throughout this process, my greatest acknowledgement must go to my patients and clients. Sometimes we are led to believe that seeking psychotherapeutic support is a sign of weakness or fragility, or is a result of a lack of resilience. But I can tell you that the people who have taught me more than any book or journal article are the people whom I have sat across from in my therapy room. Being a psychotherapist and mental health nurse has meant that I have met people in the darkest moments of their lives. While this has undeniably taken its toll on my own emotional health over the years, I still feel incredibly honoured to have been able to witness the extraordinary examples of strength and courage shown by the people I have gotten to know through my work. Children as young as six years old have shown me the meaning of resilience as they have battled, failed and gotten back up again. I would not be who I am today were it not for the privilege of being trusted to do this work with them, and so to every patient, client, service user and family member I have met along the way, thank you.